The Here's Health
Wholefood Cookery Course

Twelve delicious seasonal menus, complete with time plans and techniques of preparation, which will inspire every cook to a healthier way of eating.

CW00953164

Cookware kindly loaned by:
David Mellor, 4 Sloane Square, London SW1
Boots Household Department, at selected branches of Boots
Divertimenti, 68 Marylebone Road, London W1

The Here'sHealth
WHOLEFOOD
Cookery Course

Step-by-step guidelines for preparing a wide range of delicious wholefood menus

by

JANETTE MARSHALL AND SARAH BOUNDS

Photography by John Welburn Associates

THORSONS PUBLISHING GROUP
Wellingborough · New York

First published 1983
First paperback edition 1986

British Library Cataloguing in Publication Data

Marshall, Janette
   The Here's Health Wholefood/Cookery Course
   1. Cookery (Natural foods)
   I. Title   II. Bounds, Sarah
   641.5'637   TX741

   ISBN 0-7225-1292-9

Printed in Italy

CONTENTS

INTRODUCTION

This Cookery Course is designed to help people learn how to cook, and to teach those who can cook how to use wholefood ingredients. So, rather than starting with boiling an egg (free-range, of course), we have decided to make the course immediately useful and practical by presenting each 'lesson' in the form of a menu. Each menu is based on a theme discussed in its Nutritional Notes. This way, at the same time as learning to cook with ingredients like wholemeal flour and pasta, brown rice, pulses, carob, tofu and tahini, you are also learning about the health reasons for using them in preparing all sorts of dishes.

A time plan has been prepared for each menu, so the inexperienced cook knows when to start work in the kitchen and the order in which to proceed to make sure that everything is ready for serving at just the right moment. Many cooks will find particularly useful the menus that show how to prepare traditional foods, like Christmas turkey and Easter lamb, with a wholefood approach, but which also give delicious and original vegetarian alternatives.

However you decide to approach the Course, preparing your wholefood kitchen is an essential first step. From having the right basic ingredients at hand, to owning a sharp vegetable knife, the following guidelines will save you time, money and nutrients.

A Basic Stock Cupboard

A large part of the art of cooking and entertaining depends on a combination of using the right equipment for the job and knowing the right method of preparation for the food. It also depends on keeping your kitchen cupboard or larder stocked with the right ingredients.

The following basic ingredients will ensure that you can make a meal at any time of the day (or night). They are the 'backbone' of the menus in this cookery course, enabling the busy cook or host to concentrate on shopping for the more special, unusual or important items for the meal.

There will be some which you feel you would never need to use, more, perhaps, not on the list which you think you could never be without. It is a basic, rather than definitive, list to which, over the years, you can add and amend so that it becomes your own. The important thing is to make a start.

Baking powder

Bouillon cubes — vegetable stock cubes, unsalted.

Bread, wholemeal. If you have a freezer, batch bake and freeze your own, and if a loaf should go stale make breadcrumbs and freeze them in a bag — a great time saver.

Butter, unsalted. Soft and hard vegetable margarines high in polyunsaturated fatty acids.

Dried beans, split peas and lentils.

Flour, wholemeal.

Fruit, dried e.g., apricots, currants, sultanas (golden seedless raisins), prunes and others of your choice.

Herbs (fresh are best) e.g., sage, parsley, oregano, marjoram, thyme, fennel, dill, basil, rosemary, mint, tarragon. All these can be grown in pots indoors or in a window box if no garden space is available, but dried herbs will do if fresh are not obtainable.

Honey, clear and set.

Mayonnaise, cold-pressed varieties from health food shops.

Oil, cold-pressed olive, safflower or sunflower for salad dressings, corn, soya or sesame for cooking.

Oats, rolled.

Pasta, wholewheat e.g., spaghetti, macaroni, lasagne, shells and rings.

Rice, brown — long and short grain.

Seasonings e.g., paprika, cayenne pepper, black peppercorns (and a mill), mustard powder and ready made.

Setting agents — gelatine, agar agar.

Spices, curry spices e.g., cumin, coriander, garam masala, turmeric, allspice, juniper berries, mace and sweet spices e.g., cinnamon, mixed spice, nutmeg, cloves.

Thickening agents — arrowroot, cornflour.

Tinned tomatoes, sweetcorn, chickpeas (garbanzo beans), kidney/borlotti beans, tuna fish, anchovies etc.

Tomato ketchup, soy sauce, Worcester sauce, tahini.

Vinegar, white wine, red wine and cider/herb vinegars of choice.

Note: With the exception of tinned goods and dried pulses, most of these ingredients are best used fairly 'fresh'. Do not store them in large quantities.

Basic Equipment

Having the right utensils for the job is as essential in cooking as it is in any other skill. A tailor would not sew a ball gown with button thread and similarly if the cook is sloppy about measuring out ingredients when following recipes or, for example, does not whisk the egg whites stiff enough because he/she doesn't have a good whisk, then the final results will be disappointing.

Giving food a professional appearance is important too because it makes the food tempting, which is especially important if some of the ingredients may be unfamiliar to those eating it. Making food look good is important if it is going to be accepted and enjoyed.

Here is a list of equipment that will make life easier for the cook, cut down preparation time in the kitchen and help give more professional results.

Saucepans

Choose stainless steel in preference to aluminium. Stainless steel does not react with food. When some foods are cooked in aluminium pans the acids in them, particularly fruits and vinegary foods, react with the metal making it shiny. Whether the aluminium absorbed in the food is harmful is subject to debate, but why risk it?

Good quality (heavy) stainless steel pans may cost more than aluminium pans but they will last a lifetime. They also clean easily and look good after 20 years' wear if looked after properly. Many of the Scandinavian brands are best and they are also well designed (too good to hide in cupboards). Consider choosing pans that can also be used in the oven as casseroles and that are attractive enough for serving food in.

Cast iron French pans are also extremely useful. Because they are so heavy, with thick well-constructed bases, they conduct the heat extremely well and can be used on the stove top on the minimum gas or electric setting. With a well-fitting lid it is possible to cook a 'casserole' on top of the stove in these pans and to cut down on the amount of liquid added to food for cooking. The lids trap the steam and food cooks in its own moisture, preventing vitamins leaking out into water which may be thrown away. It is also easy to cook one-pot meals in these pans.

Good quality cast iron enamelled pans are useful, too, for slow cooking and give even heat distribution. Like glass saucepans they do not react with food.

A **double boiler** is another useful piece of equipment, but not essential because it can be improvised using a heatproof basin stood on a metal trivet (or a small piece of wood) inside a pan of boiling water. This piece of equipment is used for making sauces, custards or mixtures like lemon curd that must not boil (boiling would result in a curdled mixture). Put aside an old saucepan for this job because it will become furred by mineral deposits like the inside of a kettle. This pan can also be used for boiling eggs — do not boil eggs in saucepans used for general cooking because it will spoil them.

A pair of **scales** and a **measuring jug** are essential. There is no point in wasting expensive raw ingredients by not bothering to measure them out. Sometimes the cook might be lucky but correct weights and volumes are essential for recipes like choux pastry, soufflés and mousses. A transparent glass measuring jug that is also heatproof is very useful. Check that the pan on the scales is what you want. It may be clumsy to lift and difficult to pour from. It may also not come away from the scales very easily (check this on wall-mounted scales).

Speaking of **kettles** there are some very attractive models available which look more like ceramic coffee pots than kettles. Before you buy check the volume if you have any special needs (like an extra large/small family) and make sure it's stainless steel. Before you boil it put in only the amount of water you need; don't boil a whole kettle full for one cup of tea — it wastes fuel and money. Fill fresh from the tap each time you want water; don't keep reboiling the same old water all day!

Mixing bowls are also essential pieces of equipment. Have a large one for jobs like breadmaking and a small one for making cakes or whisking an egg white. If you have a large food mixer use that bowl for lots of jobs — don't clutter the cupboards with more than you need. Both transparent glass Pyrex bowls and the old-fashioned brown mixing bowls can be used for whisking mixtures over a pan of hot water, so it is very much personal taste as to which is chosen. When using the mixing bowl it is often helpful to place a damp cloth beneath it to prevent it slipping all over the work surface.

Ceramic basins are also useful, not only for cooking in, but also for storing left overs or stock in the fridge. They do not absorb aromas and flavours like polythene fridge containers and they can be effectively covered, leaving a headspace above the material in them, with cling film.

Spoons for the kitchen are available in many shapes and forms, often sold in attractive gift packs with a lot of other odd looking implements that will just gather dust in most kitchens. Essential to the kitchen are wooden spoons for beating and creaming mixtures and stirring food over heat. It is useful to have one for savoury mixtures that might contain garlic and another for sweet use. A tablespoon, dessertspoon and teaspoon are needed for measuring or, better still, their equivalent **plastic measures** (5, 10 and 15ml). A metal tablespoon is useful for folding egg whites into some dishes because it cuts through the mixture losing less air than a thick wooden spoon would do. A large **fork** is also handy for mixing drier mixtures or mashing, and a pliable **spatula** will enable every bit of mixture to be scraped from the sides of the bowl for economy and easier washing up.

Sharp **knives** are essential for making tasks easier and for minimizing vitamin loss (caused by damaging the things being cut by hacking with a blunt knife). The cook is also less likely to be cut using a sharp knife because less force has to be used and things are less likely to slip; it is also usual to take more care when the knives are known to be sharp.

Stainless steel knives are best and contrary to myth they can be sharpened without ruining the blade. A kitchen steel is useful, but if unsure take knives to be sharpened at a local hardware or department store. Always keep knives in a knife block, plastic wallet, cloth wrap-around or their cardboard sheaths. It is dangerous to go fumbling in drawers where upturned blades can cause nasty accidents. A carving knife, fruit and vegetable knife and palette knife are also essential for the keen cook.

Kitchen **scissors** are invaluable for cutting large quantities of herbs, topping and tailing fruits like gooseberries and red- and blackcurrants, cutting greaseproof paper to line tins, etc. A cooking **thermometer** will ensure perfect yogurt and yeast bakery. Biscuit **cutters** give a professional touch to biscuits, pastries, small pizzas etc.

A plain wooden **rolling pin,** without fancy handles, is easiest to work with and to clean. A good **sieve** is essential for light baking (to let air into the flour *not* remove the bran which should be returned to the mixing bowl) straining stocks and making *purées* if a liquidizer or food processor is not available.

A small **hand juicer** is essential for the health conscious cook. One with a strainer that catches the pips and pulp and allows the juice to fall through to a trough below is the most useful. A good **tin opener** is also essential. Choose the type that clips onto the side of the can and is worked by turning a large butterfly nut. The type that involves piercing the tin and making jagged cuts around the tin is more dangerous and messy. Wall can openers are unsightly and result in nasty splashes on the way and dropped tins.

A good **hand grater** for small amounts of fruit, vegetables and hard cheese is essential. Choose a stainless steel upright grater or a hand-held Mouli mill with a stainless steel drum. Don't forget the **colander** (a stainless steel one can also double as a steamer over a saucepan), **oven gloves** (gauntlets are best to prevent ugly and painful burns on the arm from reaching into the oven), **perforated spoon** (for skimming stocks), a **skewer** for testing whether cakes and buns and soufflés are cooked and a **fish slice** (not for frying, but to remove grilled fillets in one piece). A **timer** with a loud buzzer is invaluable, especially when baking several items at once when the dish in the oven might be forgotten while preparing another item.

Wire **cooling racks** will prevent worktops or wooden surfaces being burned or damaged by hot tins from the oven or hob. There are a great variety of **baking trays and tins** to choose from. Many are now available in stainless steel but those that are not can always be lined with greaseproof paper. To line a tin first grease the inside of the tin and then the side of the paper that will be in contact with the food. (Draw around the base of the tin to cut the lining for the bottom.) Loose-bottom tins are especially useful for cheesecakes and other soft-set mixtures; those with spring form sides make the job of unmoulding much easier. The cake can be left on the metal base and placed on the serving dish if it is too fragile to remove from the base. Non-stick tins mean that oiling is unnecessary and non-stick baking trays and bun tins are extremely easy to clean after use.

Glass or ceramic **flan dishes** and baking dishes often cut out the problem of serving dishes because they are designed for use from oven to table. A **soufflé**

dish is another useful oven-to-table dish that can also be used for baked desserts or simply as a serving dish for vegetables etc.

For roasting choose a pan with a built-in rack so the meat can be dry-roasted (i.e. without fat added). The fat will drain away from the meat into the bottom of the pan beneath the rack as the meat cooks.

Larger pieces of kitchen equipment probably are only useful if a lot of cooking is done, or if food is prepared for a large number. A **food processor** is probably the most versatile, doing anything from whisking egg whites and mixing cakes to mincing meat, chopping and slicing salads and liquidizing and blending soups. It is not so useful for smaller jobs like milling nuts which is best done just before use because nuts keep better whole. Milling exposes the oils to the air and accelerates rancidity. Nuts are easily milled in a **coffee grinder** (also useful for coffee drinkers who can buy decaffeinated coffee beans for excellent fresh coffee). A coffee grinder is also more efficient at making breadcrumbs than many food processors.

As food processors cut preparation time **pressure cookers** and **microwave ovens** cut cooking time.

A **reversible chopping board** is a good idea. Label it and use one side for vegetables such as onions and garlic which penetrate the wood easily and use the other side for 'sweet' ingredients like dried fruit and nuts which are not very nice garlic-flavoured!

Although frying is 'out' in healthy cooking, stir-frying is quite an acceptable way of serving vegetables and thin strips of meat. Stir frying is usually done in a **wok** (but a large heavy-based pan is just as effective) with the minimum of vegetable oil to prevent the vegetables sticking. An **oil well** is extremely useful for keeping down the amount of oil used. It is a small plastic container with a well of oil into which a brush is depressed. As the brush is withdrawn most of the oil is squeezed out of it so far less oil ends up in the pan than it would do when pouring from a bottle.

There are, of course, many other items available to help the cook, as a visit to one of the growing number of specialist kitchen supplies shops will reveal. Each cook has their own treasured pieces of equipment, and these will only be acquired by trial and, sometimes, error. If you are starting your *batterie de cuisine* from scratch you might like to ask an experienced cook to give you the names of their favourite make of knives, cookware etc. Or pay a visit to a large department store, or a specialist shop, and look at and handle the equipment for yourself. But remember — the prettiest and smartest-looking equipment (and there is a lot about) is not necessarily the best, although price, sadly, often *is* a reflection of quality. So expect to take your time, choose wisely and well and above all (and this goes for the whole of this Cookery Course) enjoy yourself!

Carrot Terrine. ➤

Menu 1

Italian Pasta Soup
Carrot Terrine
Mushroom Tartlets
Cinnamon Pears

Menu 1
Time plan

USE this time plan as a guide for making all, or one, of these dishes. If you plan to eat earlier or later simply put the clock back or forward on our time plan.

Mushroom Tartlets ▶

3.00 Start terrine. Cook carrots and parsnips, cook spinach and when cool mix with cheese. *Purée* carrots and parsnips together. Make sauce and stir in *purée*.

3.30 Cut leek and squash into julienne strips. Line terrine dish. Stiffly whisk the egg whites and add to sauce. Assemble terrine and bake.

4.30 Make pastry for tartlets. While chilling, cook filling. Line tins and when terrine comes out of oven, turn up oven and bake blind for ten minutes. Then fill and bake. Chill both terrine and tartlets.

6.30 Mix marzipan for pears.

6.50 Chop up ingredients for soup.

7.05 Start cooking soup.

7.10 Peel the pears and core. Stuff and bake.

7.20 Remove terrine from tin and turn out onto a bed of lettuce garnished with strips of carrot. Remove tarts from tins.

7.30 Stir in parsley and grated carrot into soup and serve immediately.

ITALIAN PASTA SOUP

Imperial (Metric)	American
1 large onion, finely chopped	*1 large onion, finely chopped*
1 clove garlic, crushed	*1 clove garlic, crushed*
2 sticks celery, finely chopped	*2 stalks celery, finely chopped*
1 tablespoonful olive oil	*1 tablespoonful olive oil*
15 oz (425g) tin tomatoes, or	*1 medium can tomatoes or 1 pound*
* 1 lb (450g) fresh tomatoes*	* fresh tomatoes*
1½ pints (900ml) stock	*3⅓ cupsful stock*
4 oz (100g) wholemeal macaroni	*1 cupful wholewheat macaroni*
1 handful chopped parsley	*1 handful chopped parsley*
2 carrots	*2 carrots*
Sea salt	*Sea salt*
Freshly ground black pepper	*Freshly ground black pepper*

Sauté the onion, garlic and celery in the oil for five minutes, without browning. Roughly chop the tomatoes, skin if using fresh. Stir in the stock and bring the mixture to the boil. Reduce heat and add macaroni, simmering for 15 minutes, until just soft. Chop the parsley and peel and grate the carrots. Stir into the soup and season to taste. Serve at once, with hot wholemeal bread.

**Everything you need for a
hearty, but not heavy soup.** ▼

**Italian Pasta Soup
Serves 4
163 calories per portion
High in fibre and vitamins.**

CARROT TERRINE

Mousse:

Imperial (Metric)	American
2 lb (900g) carrots	2 pounds carrots
8 oz (225g) parsnips	8 ounces parsnips
1 tablespoonful wholemeal flour	1 tablespoonful wholewheat flour
1 tablespoonful unsalted butter or soft vegetable margarine	1 tablespoonful unsalted butter or soft vegetable margarine
¼ pint (150ml) vegetable stock	⅔ cupful vegetable stock
2 free-range eggs, separated	2 free-range eggs, separated

Steam carrots and parsnips until just cooked. Remove from heat and drain. Make roux by stirring flour and butter together over low heat in heavy-based saucepan, stirring continuously to prevent lumps. Gradually add stock, still stirring continuously. Remove from heat and stir in egg yolks. When vegetables are cooked, *purée* and stir into roux. Whisk egg whites and add to mixture just before filling terrine.

Filling:

Imperial (Metric)	American
4 oz (100g) spinach	4 ounces spinach
Knob of butter or soft vegetable margarine	Knob of butter or soft vegetable margarine
Grated nutmeg	Grated nutmeg
2 oz (50g) low-fat soft cheese	¼ cupful low-fat soft cheese
1 leek	1 leek
1 slice pumpkin	1 slice pumpkin

Place well-washed spinach in saucepan with knob of butter and grating of nutmeg and cover with lid. Cook for three minutes. Remove from heat and when cool stir in cheese.

To build terrine:

Cut a small leek and a slice of pumpkin into julienne strips. (These are lengths of vegetables cut about half the width of potato chips.)

Line 10½-inch (26cm) terrine tin with greaseproof paper. Place layer of carrot mousse in base. Arrange three rows of squash along the length of the terrine. Cover again with a thin layer of carrot mousse and place two or three rows of leek along length of terrine. Cover again with thin layer of mousse.

Place spinach filling in piping bag with ½-inch (1cm) nozzle. Pipe two rows of filling along length of terrine and cover with rest of mousse.

Bake at 350°F/177°C (Gas Mark 4) for one hour. If using terrine tin place dish of water on shelf in oven below terrine to prevent vegetables drying out. If using ceramic or cast-iron terrine place it in a bain-marie (dish of water).

◄ **Place a layer of carrot mousse in the lined terrine and smooth the surface.**

Pipe a layer of spinach filling on top of the mousse. ▼

Carrot Terrine
Serves 6
Serve with mushroom tartlet
144 calories per portion, 567
with mushroom tartlet
High in fibre, low in fat, and full
of vitamins

MUSHROOM TARTLETS

Mushroom Tartlets
Makes 4
423 calories per tart
Low-calorie filling in wholemeal pastry

Pastry:

Imperial (Metric)	**American**
4 oz (100g) vegetable margarine	½ cupful vegetable margarine
8 oz (225g) wholemeal flour	2 cupsful wholewheat flour
Pinch sea salt	Pinch sea salt
Cold water to mix	Cold water to mix

Filling:

Imperial (Metric)	**American**
1 small onion, finely chopped	1 small onion, finely chopped
1 clove garlic, crushed	1 clove garlic, crushed
1 tablespoonful olive oil	1 tablespoonful olive oil
6 oz (175g) button mushrooms, finely chopped	2 ¼ cupsful button mushrooms, finely chopped
2 free-range eggs	2 free-range eggs
¼ pint (150ml) yogurt	⅔ cupful yogurt
1 dessertspoonful chives or chopped parsley	2 teaspoonsful chives or chopped parsley
Sea salt	Sea salt
Freshly ground black pepper	Freshly ground black pepper

Rub margarine into flour and salt until mixture resembles fine breadcrumbs. Chill for 15 minutes, meanwhile prepare the filling. *Sauté* the onion and garlic in the oil for five minutes, without browning. Stir in the mushrooms and cook for three minutes. Remove from heat and set aside. Add a little water to the chilled pastry dough, just enough to mix into a smooth, soft dough. Cut the dough into four and roll each out into a round to fit individual tartlet tins. Line with pastry and then line with greaseproof paper and baking beans, and bake blind for ten minutes at 400°F/204°C (Gas Mark 6). Remove from oven, turn down heat to 350°F/177°C (Gas Mark 4). Beat together the eggs and yogurt, season and stir into the mushroom mixture and pour into tins. Bake for 25 minutes, until firm to the touch.

CINNAMON PEARS

Imperial (Metric)
4 oz (100g) ground almonds
2 tablespoonsful lemon juice
1 teaspoonful honey
White of free-range egg, whisked
Grated orange rind
4 even-sized pears
Juice of 2 oranges
1 oz (25g) flaked almonds
Cinnamon

American
1 cupful ground almonds
2 tablespoonsful lemon juice
1 teaspoonful honey
White of free-range egg, whisked
Grated orange rind
4 even-sized pears
Juice of 2 oranges
¼ cupful slivered almonds
Cinnamon

Mix together in a bowl the ground almonds, lemon juice, honey, egg white and orange rind to make a marzipan mixture. Peel the pears and remove the cores. Stuff with marzipan and pour juice of oranges over. Sprinkle with flaked almonds and pinch of cinnamon. Bake in moderate oven at 350°F/177°C (Gas Mark 4) for about 20 minutes.

Cinnamon Pears
Serves 4
243 calories per portion
Natural marzipan adds
protein to fruit dish

▲ **Grate the rind of a well-scrubbed orange to give the marzipan a fruity flavour.**

Using a teaspoon fill the cored pears with the marzipan mixture. ➤

Nutritional Notes — Menu 1

Italian Pasta Soup is a colourful hearty soup, thick without the need for added thickeners like egg yolk, cream and flour which add extra calories too. The vegetables add fibre and vitamin C, while fresh herbs and vegetable stock boost the flavour of the soup without reliance on stock cubes with their artificial additives.

The fat level of the whole meal is kept deliberately low. Carrot Terrine requires only two eggs, far less than many similar recipes, and cream has been eliminated altogether. The high level of vegetables ensures that intake of dietary fibre and vitamin C is more than adequate. Many minerals are also present in varying amounts in these ingredients too.

Protein in the meal comes from dairy foods in the eggs, cheese, yogurt; from cereals in the wholemeal pasta and pastry and from nuts, i.e. almonds. The almonds also help to boost the level of B vitamins, as do the wholemeal pasta and pastry.

Wholemeal flour retains the goodness of the whole wheat grain. In milling of white flour the nutritious wheatgerm and vital fibre in the bran are discarded. Throwing out wheatgerm discards valuable B vitamins, vitamin E, and minerals too.

Vegetable oil and soft vegetable margarine are used in these recipes, in preference to harder animal fats such as block margarines and lard, keeping down the level of saturated fatty acids. Reliance is placed instead on polyunsaturated fats. This step is thought to be advantageous in preventing heart disease.

However, more important is the need to cut down on the total amount of fat eaten. That's why we've kept the main course light, and used yogurt in place of whole milk. Yogurt is made from skimmed milk (unless the pack states otherwise) and so is lower in fat than whole milk.

Similarly the soft cheese combined with the spinach in the terrine is a low-fat variety. We like the continental Quark now available here, rather than fatty cream cheeses.

Sugar is kept to a minimum in the stuffed pears, which rely on the natural sweetness of ingredients. Only a little honey is added — lower in calories weight for weight than pure white sugar. Honey also contains traces of minerals and vitamins too. The tanginess of orange and lemon adds extra flavour to the delicate sweet, which boosts the vitamin C level of the meal still higher.

Cookery terms used in menu 1.
Bain-marie is a shallow pan filled with hot water into which smaller pans are placed to cook without boiling or reducing. **Bake blind** is when a pastry case is baked without a filling. It is lined with greaseproof paper and filled with baking beans (any pulses will do, keep them in a specially labelled jar and use again for this purpose), then baked. This seals the pastry before fillings are added and stops large air bubbles forming which make the pastry case lose its shape. **Roux** is an equal amount of fat and flour cooked together and used to thicken sauces, etc.

Menu 2

Pink Melon Starter
Christmas Turkey (pictured below)
Piped Potatoes
Christmas Ice-cream
Chestnut Pie (alternative main course)

Menu 2   Time plan For Christmas lunch or dinner

December 23

Soak dried fruit overnight.

Christmas Eve

Make flaky pastry. This will take about an hour. Between rollings and foldings prepare the Christmas Ice-cream. Freeze ice-cream overnight and cover pastry with cling film and refrigerate.

Christmas Day

Work is arranged so that the minimum time is spent in the kitchen. Most of the work is done in two brief bursts. Two times are given for Christmas lunch or dinner.

9.30/3.30 Make the stuffings, and stuff the turkey. Place in oven, calculating cooking time to end at **1.20/7.20** by allowing 20 minutes for every 1 lb, plus 20 minutes extra.

Prepare the sprout and chestnut mixtures for the pie. Bake potato for leek and potato filling. Cook the giblets for the gravy.

11.30/5.30 Prepare the *purée* for the piped potatoes.

12.00/6.00 Prepare the leek and potato mixture for the pie. Assemble pie and bake at **12.30/6.30.**

12.30/6.30 Prepare melon starter, chilling until required.

1.00/7.00 Prepare the vegetables.

1.10/7.10 Put ice-cream in the fridge. Pipe the potatoes and bake as directed.

1.20/7.20 Make the gravy and put the vegetables on to cook.

1.30/7.30 Serve the starter.

◀USE the time plan as a guide for making all, or one, of these dishes. If you plan to eat earlier or later simply put the clock back or forward on our time plan.

Pink Melon Starter
Serves 8
100 calories per portion
Rich in vitamin C

PINK MELON STARTER

Imperial (Metric)
2 rock melons
8 oranges
4 pink grapefruit
Fresh mint

American
2 rock melons
8 oranges
4 pink grapefruit
Fresh mint

Cut melons in half and remove seeds. Scoop out melon balls and place in base of four serving dishes. Squeeze juice of two oranges and divide equally among serving dishes. Remove skin and pith from remaining six and cut flesh into segments. Remove pith from grapefruits and cut flesh into segments. Arrange segments of orange and grapefruit on top of melon balls and place one ball in the centre. Decorate with sprigs of fresh mint.

Scoop out melon balls using Parisienne cutter. ▼

Arrange fruit to represent large daisy. ▼

CHRISTMAS TURKEY

> Serves 8
> 400 calories per portion
> (5 oz/150g) meat, both stuffings
> and gravy)
> Piped potatoes serve 6; 215
> calories a portion

Imperial (Metric)	American
8-10 lb (3.6-4.5kg) turkey	*8-10 pound turkey*
Olive oil or butter	*Olive oil or butter*

If using a frozen bird, make sure it is thoroughly defrosted, following instructions on wrapper. Remove giblets and cook for gravy (page 26). Wipe bird, and wash inside the body cavity.

Stuffing the bird:

Place the mushroom stuffing in the body cavity, and the pecan parsley stuffing at the neck end, lifting the loose folds of skin. Stuff in firmly, smoothing to make a nice round shape. Cover with the skin, and tuck under the bird. Make sure the wings of the bird are tucked under the body, and tie the legs tightly across the neck. Place in roasting tin, and brush with olive oil or melted butter. Cover with foil and place in a pre-heated oven, 400°F/204°C (Gas Mark 6). Cook for 20 minutes per pound plus 20 minutes. Remove foil after one hour to nicely brown the bird, and re-cover if the bird is getting too brown. Baste with juices every half hour. At the end of the cooking time, gently tip up the bird, to let any further juices run out of the neck cavity and into the dish. Transfer to a warmed serving dish, and keep hot while making the gravy.

Pecan parsley stuffing:

Imperial (Metric)	American
2 oz (50g) pecan nuts	*½ cupful pecan nuts*
4 oz (100g) wholemeal breadcrumbs	*2 cupsful wholewheat breadcrumbs*
1 onion, finely chopped	*1 onion, finely chopped*
1 handful chopped parsley	*1 handful chopped parsley*
Sea salt	*Sea salt*
Freshly ground black pepper	*Freshly ground black pepper*
1 free-range egg, beaten	*1 free-range egg, beaten*

Grind the nuts finely and mix with the breadcrumbs, onion and parsley. Season lightly. Bind with the egg, adding a little water to moisten if required.

▲ Stuff neck cavity with pecan stuffing; place mushroom stuffing in body cavity.

▲ Pipe potato whirls using star nozzle.

Mushroom stuffing:

Imperial (Metric)
3 oz (75g) mushrooms, washed and
  finely chopped
1 onion, finely chopped
½ green pepper, finely chopped
4 oz (100g) wholemeal breadcrumbs
Sea salt
Freshly ground black pepper
1 free-range egg, beaten

American
1 cupful washed and finely chopped
  mushrooms
1 onion, finely chopped
½ green pepper, finely chopped
2 cupsful wholewheat breadcrumbs
Sea salt
Freshly ground black pepper
1 free-range egg, beaten

Mix together the chopped vegetables and the breadcrumbs, season lightly and bind with the beaten egg, adding a little water to moisten if necessary.

Gravy:

Imperial (Metric)	American
Giblets	Giblets
2½ pints (1500ml) water	6¼ cupsful water
1 onion, peeled and quartered	1 onion, peeled and quartered
1 carrot peeled and sliced	1 carrot peeled and sliced
Bouquet garni	Bouquet garni
Sea salt	Sea salt
Freshly ground black pepper	Freshly ground black pepper
Juices from the turkey	Juices from the turkey
Soya flour to thicken	Soya flour to thicken

Place the giblets in a large saucepan with the water, onion, carrot, herbs. Bring to the boil and simmer for two hours. Remove from heat and strain, discarding the giblets and vegetables. When the turkey is cooked stir in the juices — or alternatively stir the stock into the baking tin on the hob. Blend the flour with a little cold water until smooth and add to pan. Bring to the boil, stirring continuously and cook for two minutes; reduce heat and simmer gently until required.

PIPED POTATOES

Imperial (Metric)	American
1½ lb (675g) potatoes	1½ pounds potatoes
1 onion	1 onion
2 bay leaves	2 bay leaves
1 oz (25g) vegetable margarine or unsalted butter	2½ tablespoonsful vegetable margarine or unsalted butter
⅛ pint (75ml) milk, warmed	⅓ cupful milk, warmed
1 free-range egg yolk	1 free-range egg yolk

Carefully peel the potatoes, cut into pieces weighing around 1½ oz (37g) each and place in saucepan with cold water. Add the onion and bay leaves and bring to the boil. Reduce heat slightly and cook until potatoes are just soft (about 20 minutes). Strain immediately, discard onion and bay leaves and rub the potatoes through a fine sieve. Mix in the butter and the warm milk.

Fill a piping bag with the mixture, and using a star nozzle pipe spirals onto a lightly greased baking tray. Gently brush with egg yolk and place in a pre-heated oven 400°F/204°C (Gas Mark 6) for ten minutes.

Christmas fruit and nuts make a delicious mousse-textured ice-cream. ➤

CHRISTMAS ICE-CREAM

Christmas ice-cream
Serves 8
300 calories per portion

Imperial (Metric)
8 oz (225g) raisins
4 oz (100g) sultanas
4 oz (100g) dates, chopped
½ pint (300ml) apple juice
½ oz (12g) gelatine (one sachet)
Grated rind orange
Grated rind lemon
4 oz (100g) ground almonds
5 fl oz (150ml) double cream
2 free-range egg whites

American
1 ⅓ cupsful raisins
⅔ cupful golden seedless raisins
⅔ cupful chopped dates
1 ¼ cupsful apple juice
1 tablespoonful gelatine (one sachet)
Grated rind orange
Grated rind lemon
1 cupful ground almonds
⅔ cupful heavy cream
2 free-range egg whites

Soak raisins, sultanas and dates overnight in enough apple juice to cover. Next day drain fruit and add more juice to make up quantity to ½ pint (300ml/1 ⅓ cupsful). Soak gelatine in two tablespoonsful apple juice and place in bowl over pan of hot water until dissolved. When dissolved stir into rest of apple juice and place in fridge until on point of setting. Stir orange and lemon peel and ground almonds into soaked fruit. Whisk cream until just holding shape. Whisk egg whites, in separate bowl, until holding firm peaks. When apple juice is on point of setting stir into fruit mixture. Gently add cream and then add egg whites. Pour into ice-cream mould that has been wetted with cold water and place in freezer to set. Place in fridge for 30 minutes to 1 hour before serving.

CHESTNUT PIE

> **Chestnut Pie**
> **Serves 4**
> **770 calories per portion**

Wholemeal flaky pastry:

Imperial (Metric)	American
8 oz (225g) wholemeal flour	2 cupsful wholewheat flour
Pinch sea salt	Pinch sea salt
6 oz (175g) unsalted butter	¾ cupful unsalted butter
1 teaspoonful lemon juice	1 teaspoonful lemon juice
5 fl oz (150ml) ice cold water	⅔ cupful ice cold water

Sieve flour and salt into bowl. Divide fat into four and rub one-quarter into flour. Mix to dough with water and juice.

On lightly floured board roll into long oblong, keeping ends square. Place another quarter of fat in small pieces on upper two-thirds of pastry. Fold bottom third up over dough and fold top third down. Press edges lightly together to prevent air escaping and cover. Place in fridge to rest for ten minutes.

Repeat the folding and rolling twice more, adding fats as before and ensuring folded edges are on the left and right. Roll and fold once more without the addition of any fat. After final rolling rest pastry in fridge for at least ten minutes before using.

Chestnut mixture:

Imperial (Metric)	American
1 diced onion	1 diced onion
7 oz (200g) cooked and puréed chestnuts	1¾ cupsful cooked and puréed chestnuts
Wholemeal breadcrumbs	Wholewheat breadcrumbs
1 dessertspoonful freshly chopped parsley	2 teaspoonsful freshly chopped parsley
1 teaspoonful freshly chopped sage	1 teaspoonful freshly chopped sage
1 free-range egg	1 free-range egg

Sauté onion in smear of vegetable oil. Stir in chestnuts, breadcrumbs and herbs. Cool before beating in egg.

Brussels sprouts mixture:

Imperial (Metric)	American
4 oz (100g) Brussels sprouts	*4 ounces Brussels sprouts*
Knob unsalted butter or soft margarine	*Knob unsalted butter or soft margarine*
Sea salt	*Sea salt*
Grated nutmeg	*Grated nutmeg*

Prepare Brussels sprouts and steam or boil in minimum of water until just cooked. *Purée* with butter and seasoning.

Leek and potato mixture:

Imperial (Metric)	American
2 fl oz (60ml) vegetable stock	*¼ cupful vegetable stock*
2 fl oz (60ml) cream	*¼ cupful cream*
1 baked potato, sieved	*1 baked potato, sieved*
1 free-range egg, separated	*1 free-range egg, separated*
1 medium-sized potato, diced	*1 medium-sized potato, diced*
1 small leek, diced	*1 small leek, diced*

Warm stock and cream and mix with sieved potato. Beat in egg yolk. Whisk white to firm peak and fold in. Fold in vegetables.

To assemble the pie:

Line game pie mould with flaky pastry. Place chestnut mixture in the base. Spread Brussels sprouts mixture on top and finally top with leek and potato mixture. Place pastry lid in position. Seal edges and glaze with beaten egg and bake at 400°F/200°C (Gas Mark 6) for one hour.

Nutritional Notes — Menu 2

At only 100 calories a portion, melon starter is a light bright opener to the Christmas meal. The fruit is rich in vitamin C which is often lacking in winter diets.

Turkey, like other poultry and game, too is lower in calories than other meats — mainly due to its lower fat level. The fat that is present in turkey is higher in polyunsaturated fatty acids than beef, lamb and pork. Turkey supplies protein, B vitamins and minerals too. Vegetarian stuffings are lighter than the conventional sausagemeat, although pecan parsley stuffing is high in calories from the nuts.

Piped potatoes (boiled and then mashed with a little milk and butter and glazed with egg) are lower in fat than roast potatoes, and if you're in the habit of adding a lot of butter then they are also better than baked potatoes! Potatoes are also useful in boosting vitamin C intake, and they add fibre to the meal too. Sprouts and broccoli, two of the vegetables likely to be served at Christmas, also supply fibre and vitamin C plus vitamin A — particularly the broccoli — and traces of minerals.

A portion of Christmas Ice-cream sounds rich, and contains around the same calories as a portion of an average Christmas pudding — but no brandy butter or whipped cream is needed to dress up the ice-cream, so calories and fat content are in reality lower.

Chestnut Pie is a delicious vegetarian alternative to turkey. Made with wholemeal flour the pastry is more nutritious than conventional white flour because wholemeal flour retains all the goodness of the grain, including the fibre, vitamins B and E and minerals naturally present in the germ and bran which are discarded in the milling of white flour. Butter is included in the flaky pastry to add the necessary texture and to give that distinctive flavour. For everyday use it is preferable to use vegetable fats instead of animal fats, but in certain instances like this the characteristics of butter are hard to replace. Choose a soft vegetable margarine with a high level of polyunsaturates. Harder vegetable margarines contain around the same level of saturated fatty acids (the type thought unbeneficial to health) as butter. These margarines do not have a good enough flavour for flaky pastry, which should be an occasional treat. Choose unsalted butter to help keep down the level of sodium in the diet. A high intake of salt (sodium chloride) may lead to various health problems, notably high blood pressure.

The protein of the pie is made complete by the combination of nuts and grains — nuts in the form of chestnuts, the grains in the wholemeal flour and breadcrumbs. Mixing these two plant proteins together ensures that there is a good balance of the all essential amino acids needed for the body to be able to use the protein. Nuts add minerals, and B vitamins, and fibre as do the vegetables, which also contribute to the vitamin C level of the meal.

Lemon Rice Salad. ➤

Menu 3

A Day's Healthy Eating

Breakfast — Muesli
Breakfast treat — Croissants
Lunch — Lemon Rice Salad
Evening meal — Lasagne al Forno

Menu 3
Typical day's healthy eating

Breakfast

This is the meal most people base on starches. Make sure they are unrefined by choosing wholemeal bread and a wholegrain-based breakfast cereal such as sugar-free muesli with added wheatgerm.

Breakfast is also the meal when most people get their dietary fibre, that **doesn't** mean sprinkling bran on everything. A wholefood diet should not need to be supplemented with bran. Try natural yogurt or fruit juice with the muesli; if you prefer milk make it skimmed milk. Fresh fruit or dried fruit compotes make a good starter to the day.

For something more substantial try a free-range egg boiled, poached or scrambled without butter and salt.

Lunch (or light evening meal)

Whether at home or at work lunchtime is often convenient for a salad. Make sure it contains a wide variety of leaf and root vegetables, sprouted seeds and/or fruit with two of these basic proteins — nuts, pulses or cereal grains. Home-made soup or left-overs from the previous night's savouries make a change from wholemeal sandwiches in a packed lunch. Follow with fresh fruit or yogurt.

Evening (or main midday meal)

Make the main meal a protein one. Choose from lean meat, fish, poultry, free-range eggs, cheese or a combination of two of the three plant proteins — nuts, grains or pulses. This last group includes rice dishes like paella, risotto, curry or rice-stuffed vegetables. Pulses can be made into roasts (as can nuts), pâtés, vegetable stuffings. Grains include wholemeal pasta and wholemeal pastry for delicious quiches, pies and pasties.

Serve with raw vegetable salad or lightly cooked (preferably steamed) vegetables. Include green leafy vegetables if they were missing at lunchtime.

For dessert try fresh fruit, yogurt or light pudding made with wholefood ingredients such as fruit fools, pancakes, low-fat cheesecakes, mousses, crumbles.

MUESLI

Imperial (Metric)

6 oz (175g) dried fruit — apricots, figs, dates, raisins, sultanas

6 oz (175g) nuts — almonds, hazelnuts, walnuts, cashews, Brazils

8 oz (225g) porridge oats

3 oz (75g) other cereal flakes, rye, wheat or barley

1½ oz (38g) sunflower seeds, lightly toasted under a red-hot grill

American

1 cupful dried fruit — apricots, figs, dates, raisins, golden seedless raisins

1 cupful nuts — almonds, hazelnuts, English walnuts, cashews, Brazils

2 cupsful rolled oats

¾ cupful other cereal flakes, rye, wheat, or barley

⅓ cupful sunflower seeds, lightly toasted under a red-hot grill

Chop the fruit and nuts, stir into the flakes and add sunflower seeds. The mixture stores well so can be made in larger quantities as liked. Serve after soaking overnight in yogurt, orange or apple juice. Add some fresh fruit if liked.

▲ Chop a selection of fruit and nuts.

▲ Stir fruit and nuts into flakes.

Muesli
Serves 8
300 calories per portion
Mix your own sugar-free
breakfast cereal

CROISSANTS

Imperial (Metric)
1 oz (25g) fresh yeast
½ pint (300ml) tepid milk
4 fl oz (120ml) tepid water
1 teaspoonful honey
2 oz (30g) unsalted butter or
  margarine, melted and cooled
12 oz (326g) granary flour
8 oz (225g) wholemeal flour (or use
  wholemeal flour for all 20 oz)
1 teaspoonful sea salt
6 oz (175g) butter
Top of the milk

American
2½ tablespoonsful fresh yeast
1⅓ cupsful tepid milk
½ cupful tepid water
1 teaspoonful honey
¼ cupful unsalted butter or
  margarine, melted and cooled
3 cupsful granary flour
2 cupsful wholewheat flour (or use
  wholewheat flour for all 5 cupsful)
1 teaspoonful sea salt
¾ cupful butter
Top of the milk

Crumble yeast into jug and mix with tepid milk and water. Stir in the honey and the cooled, melted butter. Leave to stand. Rub the remaining butter into the flours and salt, until mixture resembles fine breadcrumbs. Make well in centre and mix in the yeast liquid, mixing in thoroughly, forming a wet dough. Cover and leave to stand until doubled in size. The mixture is now ready to use.

Divide the dough into three. Roll each third out into a circle, about ten inches across. Cut into eight equal pieces and roll up gently into a crescent shape, from the longer side, moistening the tip with a little water to stick. Transfer to a lightly oiled baking sheet and cover, leave to double for around 20 minutes. Brush gently with top of the milk and bake in a very hot oven, 425°F/218°C (Gas Mark 7) for 25 minutes until golden brown.

Croissants	**Lemon Rice Salad**
Makes 24, 118 calories each	**Serves 4, 350 calories per portion**

LEMON RICE SALAD

▲ A protein balanced salad, providing all essential amino acids

Imperial (Metric)
4 oz (100g) brown rice
1 ¾ oz (20g) pine kernels
½ oz (12g) sunflower seeds
1 tablespoonful cold-pressed
  mayonnaise
Grated rind half lemon
1 tablespoonful finely chopped
  parsley

American
½ cupful brown rice
⅓ cupful pine kernels
2 tablespoonsful sunflower seeds
1 tablespoonful cold-pressed
  mayonnaise
Grated rind half lemon
1 tablespoonful finely chopped
  parsley

To make rice balls boil rice for about 40 minutes or until cooked. Top up with water, if necessary, while cooking. Drain and cool. Stir the rice with all remaining ingredients. Form into balls by pressing between palms or hands. This is done more easily if the hands are kept wet.

Salad dressing:

Imperial (Metric)	**American**
2 tablespoonsful olive oil	*2 tablespoonsful olive oil*
1 tablespoonful lemon juice	*1 tablespoonful lemon juice*
Sea salt	*Sea salt*
Freshly ground black pepper	*Freshly ground black pepper*

Place all ingredients in clean screw-top jar and shake vigorously.

Salad base:

Imperial (Metric)	**American**
½ white cabbage	*½ white cabbage*
3 carrots	*3 carrots*
3 sticks celery	*3 stalks celery*
1 eating apple	*1 eating apple*
1 onion	*1 onion*

Grate cabbage. Scrub and grate carrots. Scrub and finely slice celery. Core and finely slice unpeeled apple. Peel and finely dice onion. Stir all ingredients together and toss in salad dressing before placing in serving bowl.

LASAGNE AL FORNO

Imperial (Metric)	**American**
1 large onion, finely chopped	*1 large onion, finely chopped*
1 green pepper, finely chopped	*1 green pepper, finely chopped*
2 cloves garlic, crushed	*2 cloves garlic, crushed*
15 oz (425g) tin tomatoes, or 1 lb (450g) fresh, skinned tomatoes	*1 medium can tomatoes, or 4 cupsful fresh, skinned tomatoes*
1 dessertspoonful fresh basil, or 1 teaspoonful dried	*2 teaspoonsful fresh basil, or 1 teaspoonful dried*
Few sprigs fresh parsley, chopped	*Few sprigs fresh parsley, chopped*
1 teaspoonful oregano	*1 teaspoonful oregano*
6 oz (175g) wholemeal lasagne	*6 ounces wholewheat lasagne*
12 oz (325g) low-fat soft cheese	*1½ cupsful low-fat soft cheese*
12 oz (325g) fresh spinach or 8 oz (225g) frozen	*12 ounces fresh spinach or 1 cupful frozen*
2 oz (50g) Mozzarella cheese	*2 ounces Mozzarella cheese*

Sauté the onion, green pepper and garlic in oil for a few minutes. Add the tomatoes, breaking them up with a spoon. Stir in the herbs and simmer gently for 20 minutes, until smooth and thick and pulped. Boil the lasagne in boiling water for 15 minutes until *al dente*. Mix together the soft cheese and spinach.

Lightly oil an oblong dish and line with pasta. Top with tomato sauce, add another layer of pasta, then spread on the spinach mixture, top with pasta, and with tomato sauce if any left. Finish with slices of Mozzarella cheese. Cover with foil and bake for one hour in a pre-heated oven 400°F/204°C (Gas Mark 6), removing foil for last ten minutes.

◀ Break tomatoes with back of spoon and cook until pulped.

Place alternate layers of tomatoes and spinach between lasagne. ▼

Lasagne Al Forno
Serves 4
334 calories per portion
Vegetarian version of a classic Italian dish

Nutritional Notes — Menu 3

Start every morning with a good breakfast to fuel your body through to lunchtime. Cut out fatty fried foods and cut down on the amount of animal products. Try mixing your own muesli (page 33) sweetened naturally with dried fruits. Our muesli is a complete meal in itself any time of day. The combination of nuts and cereal flakes makes the protein complete and there are vitamins and minerals in all the ingredients. Dietary fibre is present in the flakes, fruits, nuts and seeds too.

Granary or wholemeal croissants are a special change from wholemeal bread. Higher in fat, they are not ideal for everyday consumption — but make a lovely treat. Home-made granary flour can be made by blending wholemeal and rye flours with sprouted grains to give that characteristic nutty flavour.

At breakfast be mean when spreading the toast because it is important to try to cut down on the total level of fat in the diet. It seems advisable to switch wherever possible to soft vegetable fats and cold-pressed oils which have a higher level of polyunsaturated fatty acids than saturated fatty acids found in animal fats. In the croissant recipe, butter is important for its ability to trap air, and so make the light airy texture needed to make a good croissant. A margarine high in polyunsaturated fatty acids would not give the required texture — other margarines would have a similar amount of saturated fats as butter — without the flavour.

The remaining two meals of the day will comprise one main meal and one lighter. The lighter meal should comprise a salad of mostly raw vegetables, nuts, grains, seeds, perhaps some beans too. Dressing should not be too high in fat. The Lemon Rice Salad (page 35) gives a good amount of protein from rice, seeds and pine nuts, supplying all the essential amino acids the body needs. The vegetable base is rich in fibre, vitamins A and C with smaller amounts of B vitamins and minerals. B vitamins are supplied in greater amounts in the rice balls, which are bound with additive-free mayonnaise, lemon and parsley.

Try to cut down on the amount of animal produce you eat, particularly at the main meal of the day. Increase the amount of protein-rich plant foods such as pulses (beans and lentils), nuts and cereal grains. Make more of wholemeal products like the pasta in our meatless version of the classic Italian dish. Wholemeal pasta is higher in fibre and in B vitamins, vitamin E and other minerals than white pasta, and has a better flavour too. The lasagne is topped with a mixture of iron-rich spinach and soft cheese. Use a skimmed milk soft cheese, like the continental Quark now available in British shops, in preference to a cream cheese. Be generous with the tomatoes, onions, garlic and pepper which add colour and flavour. Top with fine slices of Italian Mozzarella cheese for an authentic topping. Serve with green salad, finish with fresh fruit.

Try to make every main meal as nutritious as possible — by increasing the amount of fresh vegetables and fruit and cutting down on fat, sugar and animal products. That way you'll bring new life to your cooking and to yourself!

Menu 4

Hummus with Melba Toast
Wholemeal Pancakes with Stir-fry Vegetables
   and Sweet and Sour Sauce (pictured below)
Apricot Mousse
Wholemeal Bread

Menu 4
Time plan

USE this time plan as a guide for making all, or one, of these dishes. If you plan to eat earlier or later simply put the clock back or forward on our time plan.

4.00 Cook apricots.

4.30 *Purée* apricots. Mix in honey and yogurt, stir in dissolved setting agent and whisk egg whites. Fold in and pour into glasses. Chill.

5.00 Cook chickpeas (garbanzo beans). While these are cooking prepare the batter for the pancakes. Make the sweet and sour sauce and remove from heat until required.

6.20 Liquidize the chickpeas (garbanzo beans) with the garlic, stir in tahini and seasonings and place in serving dish. Chill.

6.45 Prepare the vegetables for the pancake filling, but do not cook.

7.00 Make the Melba toast.

7.10 Start making the pancakes. Remove from pan and keep them hot.

7.20 Stir-fry the vegetables and quickly roll up pancakes. Keep hot in oven while eating the hummus. Reheat the sauce and pour over pancakes.

▼ **The flavour of home-made bread is unbeatable.**

HUMMUS

Imperial (Metric)	**American**
1 lb (450g) chickpeas, soaked overnight	2 cupsful garbanzo beans, soaked overnight
2 cloves garlic, peeled and chopped	2 cloves garlic, peeled and chopped
10 oz (275g) tahini	1 cupful tahini
1 teaspoonful paprika	1 teaspoonful paprika
2 teaspoonsful sea salt	2 teaspoonsful sea salt
2 teaspoonsful ground cumin	2 teaspoonsful ground cumin
Juice 2 lemons	Juice 2 lemons
Chopped parsley	Chopped parsley

Rinse chickpeas (garbanzo beans) under running cold water and place in large saucepan covered with cold water. Bring to boil, lower heat and simmer until tender (about 1 hour), topping up with boiling water as necessary. Alternatively pressure cook for 15 minutes at high pressure. When they are cooked drain and rinse with cold water. Place in liquidizer and blend to thick *purée*, adding water if necessary, pour *purée* into bowl and thoroughly mix in tahini, seasonings and lemon juice. Garnish with parsley.

▲ Mix chickpea *purée* and tahini with seasoning and lemon juice.

Prepare Melba Toast (page 44) to serve with Hummus. ►

Hummus, serves about 10 450 calories per 3 oz (75g) portion with 6 pieces of Melba toast

WHOLEMEAL PANCAKES

Stir-fry Vegetable Pancakes
Makes 10 pancakes
97 calories each with sauce

Imperial (Metric)
4 oz (100g) wholemeal flour
Pinch sea salt
1 free-range egg, beaten
½ pint (300ml) skim milk or ¼ pint
  (150ml) skim milk and ¼ pint
  (150ml) water

American
1 cupful wholewheat flour
Pinch sea salt
1 free-range egg, beaten
½ pint (300ml) skim milk or ¼ pint
  (150ml) skim milk and ¼ pint
  (150ml) water

Sieve flour and salt into mixing bowl, make well in centre and add egg and a little liquid. Stir flour into mixture working from centre towards sides of bowl. Keep paste smooth and avoid lumps by adding liquid gradually. Beat well before use.

To make pancakes lightly brush a heavy-based omelette pan with oil and heat. Pour a small amount of batter into pan and move pan to spread batter evenly over the base, keeping pancake as thin as possible. When set slip palette knife under the pancake and gently turn to cook other side. Fold pancake over and remove from pan; keep warm under low grill or in oven before stuffing.

SWEET AND SOUR SAUCE

Imperial (Metric)
4 tablespoonsful cider vinegar
4 tablespoonsful water
Juice of an orange
1 tablespoonful Demerara sugar
1 dessertspoonful tomato purée
2 tablespoonsful shoyu sauce
1 tablespoonful sherry, optional

American
4 tablespoonsful cider vinegar
4 tablespoonsful water
Juice of an orange
1 tablespoonful Demerara sugar
2 teaspoonsful tomato paste
2 tablespoonsful shoyu sauce
1 tablespoonful sherry, optional

Place all ingredients in heavy-based saucepan and place over low heat. Gently warm, stirring to prevent sticking. Add more water if mixture is too thick.

STIR-FRY VEGETABLES

Imperial (Metric)
1 onion, sliced
1 leek, washed and sliced into
   rounds
1 clove garlic, peeled and crushed,
   optional
1 green pepper, de-seeded and
   sliced into strips
2 large carrots, cut into thin strips
Few sprigs sprouting broccoli,
   divided into florets
4 large Chinese leaves, shredded
   into strips
4 handfuls beansprouts
1 small can bamboo shoots, thinly
   sliced, optional

American
1 onion, sliced
1 leek, washed and sliced into
   rounds
1 clove garlic, peeled and crushed,
   optional
1 green pepper, de-seeded and
   sliced into strips
2 large carrots, cut into thin strips
Few sprigs sprouting broccoli,
   divided into florets
4 large Chinese leaves, shredded
   into strips
4 handfuls beansprouts
1 small can bamboo shoots, thinly
   sliced, optional

Lightly brush wok or large frying pan with oil. Sesame gives a good flavour. Heat pan and add prepared onion, leek and garlic. Stir-fry to prevent burning or uneven cooking.

Cover wok and allow vegetables to cook in their own steam for two minutes. Add green pepper and carrots, stir and cook for further couple of minutes. If using bamboo shoots add next with broccoli. Cover and cook for couple of minutes.

Stir in Chinese leaves and beansprouts and continue stirring until heated through. Keep pan over low heat and take spoonfuls of mixture to fill warm pancakes. Pour over with sweet and sour sauce and serve immediately.

WHOLEMEAL BREAD

Imperial (Metric)
1 ½ lb (675g) wholemeal flour
2 teaspoonsful sea salt
1 oz (25g) soft vegetable margarine
1 oz (25g) fresh yeast
25mg vitamin C tablet, crushed
15 fl oz (450ml) tepid water
Beaten egg or milk to glaze

American
6 cupsful wholewheat flour
2 teaspoonsful sea salt
2½ tablespoonsful soft vegetable
   margarine
2½ tablespoonsful fresh yeast
25mg vitamin C tablet, crushed
2 cupsful tepid water
Beaten egg or milk to glaze

Mix flour with salt and rub in margarine. Crumble yeast into water and add the crushed vitamin C tablet. Mix well and then pour onto flour. Draw together with fingers until it forms a dough. Turn onto a lightly floured surface and knead for ten minutes, adding more flour if necessary to give a soft, smooth but not sticky dough. Cover and leave to rest for ten minutes.

Lightly grease two 1 pound loaf tins. Divide dough into two and lightly form each half into a rectangle three times the width of the tin. Fold in three and place in tin, with join underneath. Cover and leave to prove in a warm place until dough has doubled in size, about 40 minutes. Glaze with beaten egg or milk and bake in a pre-heated oven at 450°F/232°C (Gas Mark 8) for 30 minutes until golden brown, and when loaf gives a hollow sound when tapped underneath. Remove from tin and cool.

To make rolls divide the dough into 20 even-sized pieces and shape each. Place on lightly greased baking trays, cover and prove for around 20 minutes, glaze and bake at the above temperature for 15-20 minutes. Cool.

> **Wholemeal Bread**
> **Makes 2 loaves or 20 rolls**
> **100 calories per slice, 120 calories per roll**

MELBA TOAST

Wholemeal bread

Cut thick slices of wholemeal bread and toast both sides. When golden brown place on bread board and remove crusts. With sharp bread knife cut slices in half through the middle (see picture, page 41) to make two thin slices of toast.

Be careful to place one hand on top of the toast when cutting in half to prevent it slipping. Remember to work away from the body.

Place in moderate oven for 20 minutes and watch them curl into Melba toast.

APRICOT MOUSSE

Imperial (Metric)
8 oz (225g) dried apricots, soaked
  overnight in ½ pint (300ml) water
1 grated rind and juice of a lemon
1 tablespoonful clear honey (optional)
¼ pint (150ml) natural yogurt
½ oz (13g) gelatine or equivalent
  vegetable setting agent e.g. agar
  agar, carragheen
2 free-range egg whites
Blanched almonds, to decorate

American
1 ½ cupsful dried apricots, soaked
  overnight in 1 ⅓ cupsful water
1 grated rind and juice of a lemon
1 tablespoonful clear honey (optional)
⅔ cupful natural yogurt
1 tablespoonful gelatine or equivalent
  vegetable setting agent e.g. agar
  agar, carragheen
2 free-range egg whites
Blanched almonds, to decorate

Place dried apricots in pan with water, lemon juice and rind. Cook gently until soft. Liquidize and leave *purée* to cool. When cool stir in the honey if desired and the yogurt, blending in thoroughly.

Mix vegetable setting agent as directed on packet and bring to boil, then blend into *purée* at once. If using gelatine, blend with 4 tablespoonsful cold water and heat until clear. Cool and gradually add to *purée*. Stiffly whisk the egg whites and fold gently into the *purée*. Pour into four individual dishes or one large glass bowl, smoothing over the top and chill. Decorate with a few blanched almonds.

**Apricot Mousse is a light
and refreshing dessert.▼**

> **Apricot Mousse
> Serves 4
> 141 calories per portion**

Nutritional Notes — Menu 4

Wholemeal bread is probably the main item in most wholefood diets. It is the success story of the healthy eating lobby and once tasted you will understand why.

The recipe uses the Chorleywood baking process which adds vitamin C (ascorbic acid) to the yeast mixture, so the bread needs only one rising in the tin after a short ten-minute knead. This produces delicious bread in a much shorter time than the traditional double rising given to dough.

Adding vitamin C makes wholemeal bread a possibility even for the working person. It takes only 15 minutes to prepare the bread on coming home from work. Leave it to rise while the evening meal is prepared and (on the nights when a hot meal is being eaten) they can be put in the oven together.

Wholemeal bread is made from wholemeal flour that has not been refined and depleted of B vitamins, minerals, wheatgerm and its vitamin E, and bran. The bran makes the bread rich in fibre which is now known to be essential for health. The richest sources of dietary fibre are wholemeal bread, wholemeal flour and other cereal and grain products, dried pulses such as beans, peas, lentils and dried fruits.

Menu 4 is particularly rich in fibre because it uses wholemeal bread (in a sophisticated form as Melba toast); Hummus which is a delicious chickpea (garbanzo bean) and tahini *purée*; fresh vegetables and a mousse based on dried apricots.

The amount of fibre needed daily to prevent constipation and the diseases which develop from it, plus the others already mentioned, is about 35 grams. Menu 4 will provide about 20g, a substantial amount that together with a good breakfast and fruit snacks or another packed lunch will ensure an adequate amount of fibre. The fresh vegetables in the pancakes provide vitamins as well as fibre.

Wholemeal flour makes deliciously light pancakes which should not be confined to Shrove Tuesday. The same pancake recipe can also be stuffed with fruit *purées* for a fruity pudding.

At a time when fresh fruit is not plentiful making use of dried fruit is a good idea. Dried apricots are also a good source of B vitamins and iron. The apricot mousse also introduces the use of agar agar and carragheen moss. These are setting agents made from seaweed; being vegetable-based they are used in preference to gelatine by many vegetarians. If unfamiliarity has put you off using it before, have a go now, it's very simple.

As usual our menu has kept fat content low which helps keep calories down. This is important to remember when eating wholemeal bread. It is generally more filling for less calories than white bread, but the calories are often added with what goes on the bread. Remember to be mean with spreads (you don't need any with the Melba toast and moist hummus) and stick to soft vegetable fats high in polyunsaturates.

Menu 5

Vichyssoise
Cashew Stuffed Mackerel (pictured below)
Apple Crumble with Home-made Yogurt

Menu 5
Time plan

USE this time plan as a guide for making all, or one, of these dishes. If you plan to eat earlier or later simply put the clock back or forward on our time plan.

4.20 Start Vichyssoise. This will give a good two hours for the soup to chill before serving. If preferred the soup can be prepared further in advance.

6.20 Prepare stuffing for fish. Stuff the cavity in each mackerel and wrap each fish in one large, washed spinach leaf. Arrange on a bed of spinach in an ovenproof serving dish.

6.50 Rub the margarine into the flour, oats and seeds for crumble topping.

7.00 Peel and slice the apples and cook lightly. Then place in dish, cover with topping and bake.

7.05 Bake the mackerel. Allow the mackerel slightly longer than the recipe says as the oven will be lower for the crumble.

7.30 Serve Vichyssoise.

Mix stuffing ingredients and fill fish generously with stuffing. ▼

Prepare apples for crumble. They can be left unpeeled if preferred. ▼

VICHYSSOISE

Vichyssoise
Serves 6; 231 calories, or
346 calories per portion, for 4

Imperial (Metric)
2 lb (900g) leeks
1 lb (450g) potatoes
2 oz (50g) unsalted butter or soft
    vegetable margarine
2 sticks celery
1 pint (600ml) vegetable stock
¾ pint (450ml) skim milk
Sea salt
Freshly ground black pepper
Freshly grated nutmeg
¼ pint (150ml) natural yogurt

American
2 pounds leeks
1 pound potatoes
¼ cupful unsalted butter or soft
    vegetable margarine
2 stalks celery
2½ cupsful vegetable stock
2 cupsful skim milk
Sea salt
Freshly ground black pepper
Freshly grated nutmeg
⅔ cupful natural yogurt

Trim roots from leeks and split with sharp knife along length. Hold under cold running water to wash out all dirt. Slice into rounds. Scrub potatoes and roughly chop into even pieces.

Melt butter or margarine in heavy-based saucepan with well-fitting lid and place leeks and potatoes in pan. Cover and leave over low heat for about ten minutes to sweat. Scrub and coarsely chop celery and add to leek mixture. Pour over stock and milk and simmer until tender for about 25 minutes.

Leave to cool slightly before seasoning to taste and liquidize. Add yogurt and chill for two or three hours before serving.

CASHEW STUFFED MACKEREL

Imperial (Metric)
4 mackerel, cleaned but with heads
Juice of a lemon
3 oz (75g) brown rice, cooked
2 oz (50g) cashew nuts, ground
1 small onion, finely chopped
1 stick celery, finely chopped
2 tablespoonsful finely chopped
    parsley
Sea salt
Freshly ground black pepper
1 beaten free-range egg
Large spinach leaves

American
4 mackerel, cleaned but with heads
Juice of a lemon
½ cupful brown rice, cooked
½ cupful cashew nuts, ground
1 small onion, finely chopped
1 stalk celery, finely chopped
2 tablespoonsful finely chopped
    parsley
Sea salt
Freshly ground black pepper
1 beaten free-range egg
Large spinach leaves

Rub the insides of the mackerel with the lemon juice. Mix together the cooked rice, ground nuts and finely chopped onion, celery and parsley. Season and then bind together with beaten egg.

Stuff the mackerel, pressing in tightly. Wrap two spinach leaves around the fish, covering the cavity and keeping the stuffing in place. Place few leaves of spinach in base of ovenproof dish and carefully place fish on top.

Spoon over several tablespoonsful of cold water and bake at 450°F/232°C (Gas Mark 8) for 20 minutes.

**Cashew Stuffed Mackerel
Serves 4
625 calories per portion**

Wrap fish in spinach leaves to contain stuffing and moisture. ➤

APPLE CRUMBLE

Imperial (Metric)	American
3 oz (75g) wholemeal flour	¾ cupful wholewheat flour
2 oz (50g) rolled oats	½ cupful rolled oats
1 tablespoonful sunflower seeds	1 tablespoonful sunflower seeds
1 tablespoonful desiccated coconut	1 tablespoonful desiccated coconut
3 oz (75g) soft vegetable margarine	⅔ cupful soft vegetable margarine
½ teaspoonful cinnamon	½ teaspoonful cinnamon
A few cloves	A few cloves
1 oz (25g) Demerara sugar, optional	2 tablespoonsful Demerara sugar,
1½ lb (675g) cooking apples	optional
Juice of a lemon	1½ pounds cooking apples
1 tablespoonful clear honey	Juice of a lemon
	1 tablespoonful clear honey

Place flour, oats, seeds, coconut in bowl. Rub in margarine. Stir in the spices and sugar, if used. Thinly slice the apples and sprinkle with lemon juice as you do so. Place in saucepan and cook gently for two minutes.

Turn into deep ovenproof dish and dribble honey over. Cover with topping, smoothing over top and bake at 400°F/204°C (Gas Mark 6) for 20-25 minutes until fruit is tender and topping golden. Serve hot or cold with natural yogurt.

Apple Crumble
Serves 6
345 calories per portion

◄Rub in crumble mixture and place on top of the prepared fruit.

Home-made yogurt, plain or with the fruit of your choice, is easy to prepare and very economical. ➤

NATURAL YOGURT

Imperial (Metric)
1 pint (600ml) skim milk
1 tablespoonful skimmed milk
*   powder, optional*
1 tablespoonful natural yogurt

American
2½ cupsful skim milk
1 tablespoonful skimmed milk
*   powder, optional*
1 tablespoonful natural yogurt

Place milk in saucepan and heat gently to 110°F/50°C. While milk is warming mix yogurt and milk powder to a smooth paste. Pour warm milk onto paste and stir well to prevent lumps forming. Place mixture in a vacuum jug and seal. Leave to incubate for six to eight hours then place in fridge to chill thoroughly before serving.

Previous batches of home-made yogurt or bought natural yogurt can be used as starters. Most purchased natural yogurts should be 'live' i.e. contain living bacteria needed to ferment the milk sugar into lactic acid.

The bacteria are killed by heat treatment so if the carton states that the yogurt itself is sterilized, UHT (long-life) or pasteurized (don't worry if it is made from pasteurized milk since most yogurt is), then it will not contain the necessary bacteria.

The skim milk powder is added to boost the amount of 'solids' i.e. calcium, milk sugars, and proteins, making a thicker yogurt. Milk powder can be omitted for a thinner yogurt or more added for a solid set.

If using goat's milk instead of cow's milk choose a goat's milk yogurt as a starter.

Fresh fruit of choice can be stirred in before serving. Do not stir in before storing because the fruit may produce moulds in the mixture and spoil the yogurt.

> **Natural Yogurt**
> **Makes 1 pint (600ml)**
> **233 calories or 58 per 5 fl oz**
> **(150ml) portion, equivalent to**
> **small pot of yogurt**

Nutritional Notes — Menu 5

In searching for a healthy way of eating many people decide to cut down on the amount of meat they eat and find other sources of protein. For some vegetarians fish is an acceptable alternative.

Fish has a lot to offer. It may still be an 'animal' food, but the fat it contains is polyunsaturated unlike most other animal products. Polyunsaturated fatty acids (PUFAs) have been shown to have a beneficial effect on the fats in the bloodstream. Their presence helps to reduce the deposit of saturated fats as plaque, causing narrowing and hardening arteries and contributing to heart disease.

Fish, in particular oily fishes like mackerel and herring, offer special types of marine oils that make the blood less likely to form clots which cause thrombosis in the narrowed arteries. Therefore oily fishes have an important dietary role. They also contain valuable vitamins A and D.

Unlike white fish they do not need any extra oil or liquid to be added during cooking because their oil content enables them to 'cook themselves'. Wrapped in spinach to keep the steam in and prevent them from drying they make an excellent and easy meal.

Recent research has shown that the dramatic drop in the amount of fish eaten can be correlated to the rise in heart disease. Populations like the Eskimos who eat large amounts of seal meat (which also contains marine PUFAs) are free from heart disease.

Although fish provides protein it does not provide fibre; to add fibre we have included a rice and nut stuffing and a classic vegetable soup, Vichyssoise. Made from leeks this is particularly appropriate for St David's Day on March 1. It is served cold and therefore is helpful when entertaining because the host or hostess is free to chat with guests instead of quickly preparing a last-minute starter. It also makes a refreshing start to a hot meal.

Cream is traditionally used in Vichyssoise but yogurt gives it a much cleaner, tangier flavour. Another staple in the wholefood eating pattern (like wholemeal bread, see page 44, Menu 4), yogurt is very quick and easy to make at home. This ensures an additive-free product — and one which is cheaper too.

Yogurt provides the minerals (like calcium) and the vitamins found in milk but it has the health benefits of beneficial bacteria. It is the bacteria *Streptococcus thermophilus* and *Lactobacillus bulgaricus* that ferment the lactose (milk sugar) into lactic acid. This alters the pH of the milk, turning it into yogurt.

The bacteria in yogurt are thought to inhibit harmful micro-organisms in the large intestine and provide the right pH balance in which healthy gut flora can flourish. The bacteria are also thought to manufacture B vitamins in the gut helping digestion which relies on the presence of these vitamins.

Antibiotics are known to kill the beneficial bacteria in the gut and this is why natural live yogurt is given to patients who have had antibiotic treatment or gastrointestinal upsets.

The fruit crumble will add fibre to the meal in both the topping and in the fruit. The crumble topping can be used with any fruit, so use seasonal fruits to keep costs down. Serve with yogurt instead of cream for a low-calorie dessert. Using seeds and coconut helps cut down on the sugar required — you can leave sugar out altogether too. Oats and spices also contribute to the interesting texture and flavour of the topping.

Simnel Cake with Home-made Marzipan. ➤

Menu 6

Spring Vegetable Salad
Spring Lamb with Roast Potatoes
Swede and Carrot Purée
Simnel Cake with Home-made Marzipan
Bengal Black Eye Beans (alternative main course)
Vegetable Pilau

Menu 6
Time plan

USE this time plan as a guide for making all, or one, of these dishes. If you plan to eat earlier or later simply put the clock back or forward on our time plan.

4.30 Spear lamb with trussing needle and insert rosemary and garlic. Calculate cooking time, allowing 30 minutes to the pound plus 30 minutes, to end cooking at 7.30. Cook at 350°F/177°C (Gas Mark 4). Just before placing in oven prepare potatoes to roast around joint.

6.30 Cut up and peel the swede (rutabaga), slice the carrots and cook until soft. *Purée* and then reheat just before serving.

6.45 Clean, trim and then steam the asparagus and the turnips, leeks and carrots for the salad.

7.25 Cook the broccoli. Arrange the salad vegetables on a plate. Prepare the dressing and pour over the vegetables. Serve.

SPRING VEGETABLE SALAD

Imperial (Metric)
8 oz (225g) asparagus
4 baby turnips
12 baby carrots
12 baby leeks

American
8 ounces asparagus
4 baby turnips
12 baby carrots
12 baby leeks

Dressing:

Imperial (Metric)
4 tablespoonsful olive oil
2 dessertspoonsful lemon juice
1 teaspoonful ready prepared
  mustard
Finely chopped watercress leaves

American
4 tablespoonsful olive oil
4 teaspoonsful lemon juice
1 teaspoonful ready prepared
  mustard
Finely chopped watercress leaves

Wash asparagus well and using sharp knife scrape from tip to base to remove any hard, woody parts. Trim stems to uniform length and tie in bundle. Place upright in asparagus kettle (pictured) or saucepan of boiling water and cook for about 15 minutes until tender. Keep tips out of water because they will fall off if over-cooked. Drain.

Scrape turnips and carrots leaving on small stalks. Trim leeks and wash well under cold running water. Place vegetables in steamer and cook for about ten minutes until just cooked but not soft. Remove from heat and refresh under cold water. Drain.

Place dressing ingredients in screw-top jar and shake together. Arrange vegetables on plate and brush with dressing.

Spring Vegetable Salad
Serves 4
300 calories per portion

◀ Lightly steamed vegetables make
a delicious spring salad.

SPRING LAMB

Imperial (Metric)
1 leg of English lamb
1 bulb garlic
A few sprigs fresh rosemary

American
1 leg of lamb
1 bulb garlic
A few sprigs fresh rosemary

Wipe the meat and spear the flesh with a trussing needle, at two-inch (5cm) intervals. Insert rosemary and thinly sliced cloves of garlic into incisions. Place meat in roasting tin and lay on top a few more sprigs of rosemary. Cook at 350°F/177°C (Gas Mark 4) for 30 minutes to the pound plus 30 minutes.

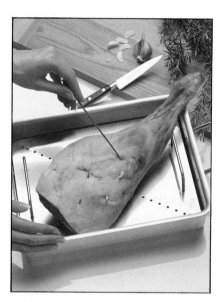

Spring Lamb
Serves 6
266 calories per 4 oz serving
Roast potatoes 166 calories, broccoli 40 calories and swede and carrot *purée* 52 calories per portion

▲Use a trussing needle to pierce the skin and insert the herbs.

Serve with lightly steamed broccoli, vegetable purée and potatoes. ➤

ROAST POTATOES

Imperial (Metric)	American
2 lb (900g) potatoes	*2 pounds potatoes*
1 oz (25g) wholemeal flour	*¼ cupful wholewheat flour*
2 tablespoonsful vegetable oil	*2 tablespoonsful vegetable oil*
Sea salt	*Sea salt*
Freshly ground black pepper	*Freshly ground black pepper*

Scrub potatoes, but do not peel. Cut into large chunks. Roast potatoes can be part boiled in boiling water for two minutes before placing in roasting dish with meat and lightly brushing with oil. Alternatively the potatoes can be rolled in seasoned flour and then placed in dish with meat and lightly brushed with oil. This coating makes them crunchy.

SWEDE AND CARROT PURÉE

Imperial (Metric)	American
2 lb (900g) swede	*2 pounds rutabaga*
12 oz (325g) carrots	*12 ounces carrots*
Knob of unsalted butter or soft	*Knob of unsalted butter or soft*
* vegetable margarine*	* vegetable margarine*
Sea salt	*Sea salt*
Freshly ground black pepper	*Freshly ground black pepper*

Cut the swede (rutabaga) into four. Peel each quarter and dice. Scrub the carrots and slice. Place in large pan of boiling water and cook until really soft, about 40 minutes. Mash well or pass through a sieve. Season and add knob of butter. Reheat and serve.

SIMNEL CAKE

Cream together the cake mixture before adding the beaten eggs. ➤

Roll out home-made marzipan for an attractive and tasty topping. ➤ ➤

Imperial (Metric)

6 oz (175g) unsalted butter or soft
   vegetable margarine
Grated rind of 2 large lemons
4 oz (100g) raisins
4 free-range eggs
1 lb (450g) wholemeal flour
1 teaspoonful baking powder
1 teaspoonful mixed spice
1 grated apple
1 lb (450g) currants
8 oz (225g) sultanas
6 oz (175g) chopped mixed peel
4 oz (100g) almonds, roughly
   chopped

American

¾ cupful unsalted butter or soft
   vegetable margarine
Grated rind of 2 large lemons
⅔ cupful raisins
4 free-range eggs
4 cupsful wholewheat flour
1 teaspoonful baking soda
1 teaspoonful mixed spice
1 grated apple
2⅔ cupsful currants
1¼ cupsful golden seedless raisins
1 cupful chopped mixed peel
¾ cupful almonds, roughly chopped

Lightly oil a deep nine- or ten-inch (23-25cm) cake tin and line with greaseproof paper by cutting a round to place on the bottom of the tin and cutting strips to line the sides. Lightly oil the paper.

Cream together margarine, grated rind of lemons and raisins. Beat eggs and gradually add to the mixture. Sieve together the flour, baking powder and spice. Stir fruit, nuts and mixed peel into flour. Gradually stir flour into egg mixture and spoon into tin evenly.

Bake in the centre of a pre-heated oven at 350°F/177°C (Gas Mark 4) for 1½ to 2 hours. If the top of the cake browns too much cover with a layer of brown paper.

Simnel Cake
Serves 16
365 calories per slice or
255 calories without marzipan

MARZIPAN

Imperial (Metric)	**American**
6 oz (175g) Demerara sugar	*1 cupful Demerara sugar*
8 oz (225g) ground almonds	*2 cupsful ground almonds*
White of large free-range egg	*White of large free-range egg*
Juice of half a lemon	*Juice of half a lemon*

Place sugar in coffee grinder or liquidizer and grind to a fine powder. Mix with ground almonds. Lightly whisk the egg white and add to mixture. Add enough lemon juice to make a paste and knead lightly until smooth.

The dark colour of natural marzipan comes from the sugar. We also used unblanched almonds for grinding. This will boost fibre content as well as darken the marzipan.

To Decorate
Roll just over half of the paste into a circle and cut it to shape by tracing round the bottom of the cake tin. Brush the top of the cake with a thin layer of apricot jam and place the marzipan in place.

Form the rest of the marzipan into egg-shaped balls. Traditionally 11 are made to represent the Apostles, excluding Judas. Fix in place on top of cake using a little jam to stick.

BENGAL BLACK EYE BEANS

Imperial (Metric)

8 oz (225g) black eye beans, soaked
  overnight
2 onions, finely chopped
1 green chilli, finely chopped
1-inch (2.5cm) fresh ginger, grated
2 black cardamoms
6 black peppercorns
1-inch (2.5cm) cinnamon stick
6 cloves
1 tablespoonful vegetable oil
4 cloves garlic, finely chopped
½ teaspoonful paprika
1 teaspoonful turmeric
½ teaspoonful ground cumin
2 teaspoonsful ground coriander
1 tablespoonful finely chopped fresh
  coriander leaves
1 teaspoonful garam masala
3 tablespoonsful lemon juice

American

1 cupful black eye beans, soaked
  overnight
2 onions, finely chopped
1 green chilli, finely chopped
1-inch fresh ginger, grated
2 black cardamoms
6 black peppercorns
1-inch cinnamon stick
6 cloves
1 tablespoonful vegetable oil
4 cloves garlic, finely chopped
½ teaspoonful paprika
1 teaspoonful turmeric
½ teaspoonful ground cumin
2 teaspoonsful ground coriander
1 tablespoonful finely chopped fresh
  cilantro
1 teaspoonful garam masala
3 tablespoonsful lemon juice

Place beans in saucepan with half the onion, and the following six ingredients, cover with cold water. Bring to the boil and then simmer till tender, about 50 minutes. Drain and keep the stock. Place the oil in a pan and cook the onion and garlic for two minutes. Add the paprika, turmeric, cumin and coriander. Stir together well. Add the drained beans and stir gently. Mix in the coriander leaves (cilantro), garam masala and lemon juice and then add sufficient stock to make a sauce, simmer gently and then serve with rice.

VEGETABLE PILAU

Imperial (Metric)
1-inch (2.5cm) fresh ginger, grated
2 green chillies, de-seeded, finely chopped
1 tablespoonful chopped coriander leaves
½ teaspoonful turmeric
1 tablespoonful vegetable oil
1 onion, finely chopped
1 teaspoonful garam masala
8 oz (225g) long-grain brown rice
1 teaspoonful cumin seeds
1 cauliflower, cut into florets
8 oz (225g) carrots, diced
8 oz (225g) tomatoes, skinned and roughly chopped
1 pint (600ml) vegetable stock or water

American
1-inch piece fresh ginger, grated
2 green chillies, de-seeded, finely chopped
1 tablespoonful chopped cilantro
½ teaspoonful turmeric
1 tablespoonful vegetable oil
1 onion, finely chopped
1 teaspoonful garam masala
1 cupful long-grain brown rice
1 teaspoonful cumin seeds
1 cauliflower, cut into florets
1¼ cupful diced carrot
1¼ cupful skinned and roughly chopped tomatoes
2½ cupsful vegetable stock or water

Grind the ginger, chillies and coriander leaves (cilantro) with the turmeric. Fry this paste in the oil, adding the onion and garam masala. Cook for two minutes and then add the rice. Stir well into mixture and when the grains are opaque, add the cumin seeds, cauliflower, carrots and tomato. Stir thoroughly and then add the stock. Bring to the boil, then reduce heat and simmer for 30 minutes until the rice and vegetables are tender, adding more water if required.

● Serve with freshly sliced bananas tossed in natural, unsweetened yogurt, lemon juice and honey and a cucumber, spring onion and green pepper salad tossed in seasoned lemon juice.

◄ **Bengal Black Eye Beans with Vegetable Pilau and side dishes**

Serves 4
558 calories per portion

Nutritional Notes — Menu 6

If the weather is kind April is the month when we can expect the first of the early spring vegetables. New baby carrots, baby turnips and baby leeks will be available to the home grower and from better greengrocers. Although May 1 is the official date for home-grown asparagus it is available from mid-April in good years.

After a winter of salads made from stored root vegetables it is important to take advantage of the fresh spring produce which provides a welcome new source of vitamin C.

Sprouting broccoli is also available from April and this makes a delicious accompaniment to British lamb traditionally eaten at Easter.

Although a healthy eating pattern means cutting down on meat, lamb or white meat are occasionally eaten. Free-range poultry and meat are the first choice because they offer more protein than other meats for less saturated fat and therefore fewer calories. Lamb is a younger meat than other red meats and therefore it will not have had time to build up residues of hormone drugs (used by farmers to increase body weight) in its body fat.

Protein is used to build and repair body cells. When more protein than is required is eaten it is broken down into energy (usually carbohydrates and fats provide energy) and one of the by-products of this conversion is uric acid. Too much uric acid can accumulate in the body and aggravate rheumatic joints and gout.

As vegetarians and vegans prove, daily meat is not necessary for health, but it does provide some of the B vitamins and is an important source of vitamin B12 which is vital for health. Meat is also a good source of iron.

Vegetarians obtain their vitamin B12 from some fermented yeast products, seaweeds, brewer's yeast and dietary supplements.

Many vegetarians successfully obtain their protein from non-animal sources such as cereal grains, pulses, nuts and seeds. Our alternative main course is based on beans. As a curry it is usually eaten with brown rice and this combination gives the body the complete range of essential amino acids to make protein. Making sure a meal contains two of the three basic vegetable protein groups (nuts, pulses or cereal grains) will ensure the protein is complete. These vegetable protein foods are also good sources of dietary fibre and with the exception of nuts, are lower in fat than fibreless meat.

Simnel cakes are traditional at Easter but they need not contain a lot of sugar. The natural sweetness in the dried fruit of a rich fruit cake negates any need for sugar. Marzipan is traditionally put in the centre of the cake before it is baked and also used to decorate the top; but this is optional and could be used either on top or in the centre. We have given a marzipan recipe which is free from the usual artificial colouring and flavouring used in many shop-bought marzipans. This cake recipe could also be used on other special occasions.

Menu 7

Avocado and Tofu Dip with Crudités
(pictured below)
Mushroom Gougère
Kiwifruit Sorbet
Courgette and Raisin Cous Cous
(alternative main course)

Menu 7
Time plan

Use this time plan to prepare the meal based on either Mushroom Gougère or Cous Cous (pictured below).

Previous night put chickpeas (garbanzo beans) in cold water to soak.

12.00 Start sorbet. Dissolve the fructose in water and cool. Peel and chop the kiwifruit and blend with fructose syrup. Sieve and freeze.

4.30 Break up frozen mixture with fork and beat until smooth. Stiffly whisk the egg whites and fold in. Freeze.

5.00 Put chickpeas (garbanzo beans) onto cook if serving cous cous. (Alternatively pressure cook at 6.00pm.)

6.30 Light oven for gougère 425°F/232°C (Gas Mark 7). Make choux pastry for gougère. At end of baking turn down heat and keep warm until ready to serve.

or Prepare sauce by *sautéing* onion, garlic and spices in olive oil for five minutes. Add tomatoes and simmer. Soak cous cous or dry roast bulghur wheat if using.

6.45 Put cous cous on to cook above chickpea (garbanzo bean) sauce.

6.50 Drain the tofu and make avocado dip. Chill, covered until required.

7.05 Prepare the mushroom sauce for gougère. Remove from heat when ready, and thoroughly reheat when ready to serve.

7.20 If serving gougère put new potatoes on to boil.

7.25 Cut up vegetables for dip.

7.30 If serving gougère, start to steam greens. Serve dip.

AVOCADO AND TOFU DIP

> **Avocado and Tofu Dip**
> **Serves 4**
> **170 calories per portion, including crudités**

Imperial (Metric)
10 oz (275g) tofu
2 large ripe avocados
Juice of half a lemon
Freshly ground black pepper

American
1 ⅔ cupsful tofu
2 large ripe avocados
Juice of half a lemon
Freshly ground black pepper

Crudités:

Imperial (Metric)
½ cucumber
4 sticks celery
Green pepper
Red pepper

American
½ cucumber
4 stalks celery
Green pepper
Red pepper

Drain the tofu and cut into cubes. Place in mixing bowl. Halve the avocados and scoop out the flesh. Add to tofu and sprinkle with lemon juice to prevent discolouration.

Beat together the tofu and avocado to make a soft dip. Season to taste with freshly ground black pepper.

Prepare crudités by cutting even-length strips of the vegetables and arrange around the avocado dip.

▼ **Scoop flesh from halved avocados.**   ▼ **Slice crudités just before serving.**

MUSHROOM GOUGÈRE

Mushroom Gougère
Serves 4
350 calories per portion

Gougère is made from choux pastry, a useful addition to a wholefood cook's repertoire. 100 per cent wholemeal flour tends to rise less well — so you could use 85 per cent wholemeal flour (or sieved 100 per cent) for a lighter pastry. 81 or 85 per cent flours retain the vitamin and mineral-rich wheatgerm but the bran particles have been sieved out, so it is not the ideal choice for everyday baking.

Imperial (Metric)	American
2 oz (50g) soft vegetable margarine	¼ cupful soft vegetable margarine
¼ pint (150ml) cold water	⅔ cupful cold water
2½ oz (65g) 85 per cent wholemeal flour	⅔ cupful 85 per cent wholewheat flour
2 free-range eggs	2 free-range eggs
2 oz (50g) Gruyère cheese, grated	½ cupful grated Gruyère cheese
Pinch mustard	Pinch mustard
Freshly ground black pepper	Freshly ground black pepper

Sauce:

Imperial (Metric)	American
1 oz (25g) soft vegetable margarine	2½ tablespoonsful soft vegetable margarine
1 oz (25g) wholemeal flour	¼ cupful wholewheat flour
¼ pint (150ml) skim milk	⅔ cupful skim milk
¼ pint (150ml) vegetable stock	⅔ cupful vegetable stock
1 large onion	1 large onion
8 oz (225g) button mushrooms	4 cupsful button mushrooms
Pinch thyme	Pinch thyme

Place margarine and water in medium-size pan. Heat until margarine has melted and liquid is boiling. Quickly shoot sieved flour into pan. Remove from heat and immediately beat flour into mixture. Continue beating until mixture leaves sides of pan. The choux paste should be smooth and glossy.

Beat in one egg and continue beating until no traces of egg remain. Add the second egg and again beat until thoroughly blended in. Finally beat in the grated cheese and seasoning.

Lightly grease an oval dish, ten inches (25cm) long. Pipe spirals of mixture around sides. Bake in a pre-heated oven at 425°F/232°C (Gas Mark 7) for 20 minutes, then reduce heat to 375°F/190°C (Gas Mark 5) for a further ten minutes. The choux ring should then be quite firm, golden in colour and well-risen.

While the pastry is baking prepare the filling. Melt the margarine in a pan and stir in the onion, cook for two minutes. Stir in the sliced mushrooms and cook a further two minutes. Remove from pan draining off the juices and fat. Add a further ½ oz (12g) margarine to pan and melt. Stir in the flour and cook gently for a minute, beating together. Gradually stir in the milk and stock over a low heat. Bring to the boil and then reduce heat to a simmer. Stir in the onions and mushrooms and season. Keep heating gently until choux pastry is ready and then pour into the centre of the ring and serve immediately.

▲ Beat choux pastry well.   ▲ Pipe pastry into dish for gougère.

KIWIFRUIT SORBET

Imperial (Metric)
2 oz (50g) fructose
¼ pint (150ml) cold water
5 kiwifruit
2 free-range egg whites

American
⅓ cupful fructose
⅔ cupful cold water
5 kiwifruit
2 free-range egg whites

Place the fructose and water in a small saucepan and heat gently until the sugar has dissolved. Boil for one minute and remove from heat. Leave to cool.

Gently peel the kiwifruit and roughly chop. Place in a blender goblet with the cool syrup and blend till smooth. Sieve the *purée* to remove the pips (leave them in the mixture if preferred). Transfer to a shallow polythene container and freeze for three to four hours until just mushy.

Beat with a fork to break up any ice crystals. Stiffly whisk the egg whites and gently fold into the fruit mixture with a metal spoon. Return to the freezer and freeze until firm — about three hours. Spoon or use a scoop and serve in four individual glasses.

Fresh fruit sorbets make sophisticated and refreshing desserts. ▼

**Kiwifruit Sorbet
Serves 4
100 calories per portion**

COURGETTE AND RAISIN COUS COUS

Imperial (Metric)
8 oz (225g) chickpeas, soaked
  overnight
2 onions, diced
2 cloves garlic, crushed
1 tablespoonful freshly grated ginger
½ teaspoonful freshly ground black
  pepper
¼ teaspoonful ground cumin
1 tablespoonful olive oil
2 lb (450g) fresh tomatoes or
  2 × 14 oz (400g) tins
Vegetable stock
12 oz (325g) cous cous
2 large courgettes
2 oz (50g) raisins

American
1 cupful garbanzo beans, soaked
  overnight
2 onions, diced
2 cloves garlic, crushed
1 tablespoonful freshly grated ginger
½ teaspoonful freshly ground black
  pepper
¼ teaspoonful ground cumin
1 tablespoonful olive oil
2 pounds fresh tomatoes or 2
  medium cans
Vegetable stock
12 ounces cous cous
2 large zucchini
⅓ cupful raisins

Drain soaked chickpeas (garbanzo beans) and boil for 1½ hours or cook for 30 minutes in a pressure cooker at high pressure. When they are almost ready, *sauté* onions, garlic and spices in olive oil for five minutes over a low heat. If using fresh tomatoes dice roughly before adding to mixture, break up tomatoes with back of wooden spoon and add partly-cooked chickpeas (garbanzo beans). Cover and simmer.

Pre-soak the cous cous according to instructions on pack.

Thinly slice the courgettes (zucchini) and mix in with the soaked cous cous when it has swelled. Stir in the raisins and place the mixture in the top of a *couscousier*. If this is not available line a stainless steel colander that will sit inside the rim of the saucepan containing the chickpea (garbanzo bean) mixture, with muslin and place the cous cous mixture in this. Place cous cous over the top of the simmering sauce, and continue cooking until the sauce is ready — about 40 minutes.

Turn cous cous onto serving dish and pour over sauce.

**Courgette and Raisin
Cous Cous
Serves 4
430 calories per portion**

Nutritional Notes — Menu 7

Wholefood cookery brings together healthy ingredients from many different countries of the world. In Menu 7 we have combined tofu from the Far East with cous cous from the countries of North Africa together with New Zealand's kiwifruit, Israel's avocado pears and gougère (using Swiss cheese) from France.

Tofu has been used in Japan and China for centuries. Produced from soyabeans the beans are first soaked, then *puréed* and are then separated into curds and whey by the addition of either a salt or acid. The process is similar to the production of cheese from milk. The soyabean curds are finally pressed and the result is tofu.

Tofu has a very low fat content (only three per cent fat) and supplies protein which, coming from the bean, should be balanced with either grains or nuts or with animal proteins. In this instance the tofu dip is served before either the gougère (with wheat, eggs and cheese) or cous cous (with wheat and bean proteins). Tofu is also a good source of calcium and supplies other minerals and vitamins too.

Although avocados supply potassium and other minerals as well as vitamins C, B and E, they are quite oily. This makes them higher in calories than many fruits and vegetables, but the oils are polyunsaturated and unsaturated rather than the less desirable saturated fats.

Gruyère cheese is so strongly flavoured that only 2 ounces (50g) is needed to give a rich, cheesy tasting pastry. This helps keep down the calories. Omit the cheese and seasoning and you have choux pastry for sweet dishes but go easy on the fat and calorie-rich double cream and chocolate usually used in eclairs and profiteroles. Choose instead low-fat soft cheese either alone or mixed with fresh or dried fruit *purée* or, for a savoury filling, mix the cheese with spinach.

Cous cous is an alternative main course for Menu 7. It is used in North African countries, produced from semolina. The tiny grains are rolled together to make slightly larger particles of cous cous. Cous cous is sold pre-cooked so needs only a short soak before finishing cooking in the traditional *couscousier* over a sauce of chickpeas (garbanzo beans) and vegetables.

Chickpeas (garbanzo beans), being a pulse, balance the protein in the wheat-based cous cous. Cracked wheat or bulghur can be used as an alternative to cous cous. These are made from the whole wheat grain, whereas cous cous is made from refined semolina, and so they are a healthier alternative. Dry-roast bulghur for two to three minutes before cooking.

Kiwifruits, rich in vitamin C and low in calories (only 30 calories each), make a lovely end to a meal. Tasting somewhere between a watermelon and strawberry their pale green flesh makes a striking contrast when used in fruit salads. *Puréed* they make a delicate sorbet.

Fructose sweetens our sorbet. Although it looks like white granulated sugar (sucrose) it is a healthier alternative. Fructose, or fruit sugar, is sweeter than sucrose so less needs to be used in recipes — saving calories.

Menu 8

Cauliflower and Fennel Soup with a Pastry Lid
Smoked Trout Mousse (pictured below)
Tomato Salad
Carob Chip Cookies
Vegetable Pasties (alternative main course)

Menu 8

Time plan

USE this time plan as a guide for making all, or one, of these dishes. If you plan to eat earlier or later simply put the clock back or forward on our time plan.

4.50 Start smoked trout mousse. Flake fish and mix with soft cheese and yogurt, lemon juice, onion and seasoning. Dissolve gelatine and add to mixture. Stiffly whisk egg whites, fold in and pile into wetted fish mould. Chill.

5.30 Make cookies. Pre-heat oven to 375°F/190°C (Gas Mark 5). Cream margarine and honey, beat in egg and stir in chopped nuts, carob and sunflower seeds and flour. Place spoonsful of mixture on a lightly greased baking tray and bake. Continue baking rest of mixture in batches.

6.25 Cook cauliflower for soup and prepare fennel and onion sauce. Liquidize both and reheat, thinning if necessary.

6.50 Turn oven up to 400°F/ 204°C (Gas Mark 6). Rub fat into flour for pastry topping. Stir in fennel seeds and roll out. Cut out to fit top of ovenproof bowl. Pour soup into serving dishes and top with pastry lid. Glaze the top and bake for 20 minutes.

7.15 Prepare cucumber and tomato salad.

7.30 Serve soup.

CAULIFLOWER AND FENNEL SOUP

> **Cauliflower and Fennel Soup**
> **Serves 4 for lunch, 6 as starter**
> **240 calories per portion for four**
> **160 calories for six**

Imperial (Metric)	American
1½ lb (675g) cauliflower	1½ pounds cauliflower
6 oz (175g) fennel, diced	6 ounces fennel, diced
1 onion, diced	1 onion, diced
1 tablespoonful sunflower oil	1 tablespoonful sunflower oil
1 tablespoonful wholemeal flour	1 tablespoonful wholewheat flour
1 teaspoonful ready-made stoneground mustard	1 teaspoonful ready-made stoneground mustard
1 vegetable bouillon (stock) cube	1 vegetable bouillon (stock) cube

Wash cauliflower and place whole head in saucepan with about two inches of boiling water in the base. Cover and leave to cook for ten minutes.

Meanwhile set oven to 400°F/204°C (Gas Mark 6). Place fennel and onion in heavy-based saucepan with the oil and cover. Leave to sweat for five minutes. Stir in the flour and mustard to coat the onion and fennel. Gradually add the water from the cooked cauliflower to make a smooth sauce.

Place cauliflower and sauce on one side to cool. Remove from heat and roughly chop the cooked cauliflower. Liquidize the cauliflower and the fennel and onion mixture and return both to one of the saucepans. Thin, if necessary, with stock.

Pastry lid:

Imperial (Metric)	American
4 oz (100g) wholemeal flour	1 cupful wholewheat flour
1 oz (25g) soft vegetable margarine	2½ tablespoonsful soft vegetable margarine
1 oz (25g) mature English Cheddar, grated	¼ cupful grated mature Cheddar
1 teaspoonful fennel seeds	1 teaspoonful fennel seeds
Beaten free-range egg for glazing	Beaten free-range egg for glazing

Make the pastry by sieving the flour into a mixing bowl. Add the margarine and rub in until the mixture resembles breadcrumbs. Stir in the fennel seeds and cheese and roll out. Cut out lids by using the tops of the ovenproof soup bowl or ramekins as a cutter.

Pour the soup into the bowls and glaze the inside edge of the pastry lid (to help it stick to the soup bowl rim). Place in position and glaze the top. Bake at once for 15-20 minutes until pastry is golden brown.

SMOKED TROUT MOUSSE

Imperial (Metric)	American
10 oz (275g) smoked trout	10 ounces smoked trout
8 oz (225g) low-fat soft cheese	1 cupful low-fat soft cheese
Juice of half a lemon	Juice of half a lemon
2 oz (50g) finely chopped onion	1/3 cupful finely chopped onion
8 fl oz (240ml) natural yogurt	1 cupful natural yogurt
Sea salt	Sea salt
Freshly ground black pepper	Freshly ground black pepper
1/2 oz (12g) gelatine	1 tablespoonful gelatine
4 tablespoonsful cold water	4 tablespoonsful cold water
2 egg whites	2 egg whites
Cucumber to garnish	Cucumber to garnish

Remove skin and bones from fish and flake finely. Mix with the soft cheese until well blended. Stir in the lemon juice, finely chopped onion and the natural yogurt. Season.

Blend the gelatine with the cold water and heat gently until the gelatine has dissolved. Cool. Beat gelatine into fish mixture gradually, making sure it is thoroughly mixed in. Stiffly whisk the egg whites and gently fold into the mixture with a metal spoon. Smooth mixture into a wetted mould and place in fridge to set.

To turn out, dip mould in hot water and squeeze sides of mould. Quickly turn out onto a bed of finely sliced cucumber. Serve with a salad like tomato salad and with wholemeal bread.

TOMATO SALAD

Imperial (Metric)	American
1 lb (450g) tomatoes	1 pound tomatoes
1 small onion	1 small onion
2 tablespoonsful fresh parsley, basil or chives, finely chopped	2 tablespoonsful fresh parsley, basil or chives, finely chopped
3 tablespoonsful olive oil	3 tablespoonsful olive oil
1 tablespoonful white wine vinegar	1 tablespoonful white wine vinegar
Sea salt	Sea salt
Freshly ground black pepper	Freshly ground black pepper

Finely slice the tomatoes and onion. Arrange in a dish in overlapping circles. In a screw-top jar shake together the herbs, oil, vinegar, and seasoning. Pour over tomatoes and onions.

| Smoked Trout Mousse
Serves 4
220 calories per portion | Carob Chip Cookies
Makes 30 cookies
90 calories per biscuit |

CAROB CHIP COOKIES

Imperial (Metric)
4 oz (100g) soft vegetable margarine
6 tablespoonsful clear honey
1 free-range egg
3 oz (75g) chopped walnuts
1½ oz (40g) lightly toasted
    sunflower seeds
3 oz (75g) carob bar, finely chopped
6 oz (175g) self-raising wholemeal
    flour

American
½ cupful soft vegetable margarine
6 tablespoonsful clear honey
1 free-range egg
⅔ cupful chopped English walnuts
⅓ cupful lightly toasted sunflower
    seeds
3 ounce carob bar, finely chopped
1½ cupsful self-raising wholewheat
    flour

Cream the margarine and honey until thoroughly blended and light. Beat in the egg. Fold in the chopped nuts, sunflower seeds and chopped carob bar with the flour and mix lightly until thoroughly blended.

Place small spoonsful of the mixture on a lightly greased baking tray, well apart Bake at 375°F/190°C (Gas Mark 5) for 15 minutes until golden brown. Transfer to a wire cooling tray where they will crisp up as they cool. ▼

VEGETABLE PASTIES

Vegetable Pasties
Makes 5
380 calories per pasty

Imperial (Metric)
12 oz (325g) wholemeal flour
6 oz (175g) soft vegetable margarine
Pinch sea salt
Cold water to mix
1 lb (450g) of finely diced seasonal
   vegetables. We used carrots,
   cauliflower, onion, mushroom,
   sweetcorn, potato
1 tablespoonful water
Pinch thyme
Sea salt
Freshly ground black pepper
Beaten free-range egg to glaze

American
3 cupsful wholewheat flour
¾ cupful soft vegetable margarine
Pinch sea salt
Cold water to mix
1 pound of finely diced seasonal
   vegetables. We used carrots,
   cauliflower, onion, mushroom,
   sweetcorn, potato
1 tablespoonful water
Pinch thyme
Sea salt
Freshly ground black pepper
Beaten free-range egg to glaze

Light oven 400°F/204°C (Gas Mark 6). Rub fat into flour and salt until mixture resembles fine breadcrumbs. Chill for ten minutes. Add enough cold water to mix to a dough. Cut dough into five and roll each piece out to a rough circle. Using a side plate or plain flan ring as a guide, cut out circles.

Mix chopped vegetables together in a bowl and stir in water, thyme and a little seasoning. Place filling along the centre of each pastry circle. Using a pastry brush lightly dampen edges of circle. Bring the pastry together to meet over the filling and squeeze edges together to seal.

Using the back of a knife flute the edges. Glaze with beaten egg and bake for 20-25 minutes until pastry is golden brown.

Nutritional Notes — Menu 8

An ideal main course for summer months is Smoked Trout Mousse. Served chilled with accompanying salads the mousse is light textured but not too rich. Yogurt and low-fat soft cheese replace the double cream and rich sauce usually used to form the basis of savoury mousses, reducing the fat content of the dish and the calorie count too.

We used smoked trout, but other smoked fish (mackerel, cod or haddock) or canned tuna could be substituted. Smoked trout, like smoked mackerel, is hot smoked to preserve the flesh, and give it that distinctive flavour. By-products of the smoke inhibit the growth of microorganisms and so extend shelf-life. The process cooks the flesh so both fish can be used without further cooking. Cold smoking used for smoked cod, haddock and for kippers does not cook the flesh so these all need subsequent cooking. While some processors do add colourings to smoked products, not all do. It is the bright yellow smoked cod and haddock that are more likely to contain colourings rather than the pale coloured flesh of smoked trout and mackerel. Finnan haddock is free from additives.

Although trout is classified as an oily fish rather than a white fish, it is much lower in fat than mackerel and herring, containing only three per cent fat compared to 16 and 18 per cent fat found in mackerel and herring respectively. This makes it lower in calories too. As trout farms have become more widespread in recent years it is now easy to buy reasonably priced fresh and smoked trout.

While mousse and salads are ideal for warm summer days, the British climate means that warm days are interspersed with cooler days. Cauliflower and fennel soup would make an ideal lunch for such a day or could be served in smaller dishes to make an unusual starter. Florence fennel has a sweet, slightly aniseed flavour and a pale colour which complements that of cauliflower. *Puréed* together the result is a super smooth, pale soup. Cheese and fennel seeds make a tasty pastry to top the serving bowls — remember to use ovenproof dishes, as the pastry topping needs cooking.

Pastry is used in many traditional British dishes. Cornish pasties need not be for meat eaters alone — mix together a selection of finely chopped vegetables to make a more nutritious filling. Choose seasonal produce; winter root vegetables are just as suitable as some of summer's lighter produce. Roll out pastry circles (slightly smaller for younger children's lunch boxes) and add 2 ounces (50g) grated Cheddar to the filling for extra protein, if liked.

Carob chip cookies are another favourite with children and equally suitable for summer picnics and lunch boxes. To finish off a meal serve a plateful of cookies with a selection of fresh fruit or with natural yogurt. Sweetened with honey which contains some vitamins and minerals and is naturally sweeter than refined sugars, the cookies substitute carob chips for chocolate. Carob, which comes from the pod of the carob tree, has several nutritional advantages over chocolate. It is lower in calories, lower in fat, naturally sweeter, contains five times as much iron, less sodium and more potassium. It is also free of caffeine and theobromine — two stimulants in chocolate which can prove addictive and trigger attacks of migraine.

Carob can be bought either as a powder (see menu 12) or as a bar. A finely chopped carob bar is mixed with chopped walnuts and lightly toasted sunflower seeds to give a cookie with an interesting 'crunch' and flavour.

▼ **Enjoy the delicate flavour and colour of Smoked Trout Mousse (page 76).**

Menu 9

Black Olive Pâté
Picnic Pizzas
Pan Bagnat
Hummus Stick
Cheese Baps
Green Salad
Light Lemon Cheesecake

Menu 9
Time plan

This menu is ideal for a mid-summer picnic or for a buffet lunch in the garden. Follow our time plan to make light of the preparation so you're ready to leave for your picnic, or alternatively to serve lunch, at 1.00pm.

9.00 Make tomato sauce for pizzas.

9.15 Make up 3 lb (1.5k) batch of dough to make pizzas and two bagnats. Cover and rest for ten minutes.

9.40 Pre-heat oven to 425°F/ 232°C (Gas Mark 7). Divide the dough into three. Shape two thirds into bagnats. Cover and leave to prove for about 40 minutes. Roll out remaining third and cut out rounds for pizzas. Top with sauce and chosen topping. Prove for ten minutes, then bake.

10.00 Make dough for baps.

10.15 Bake bagnats if ready. Oil loose-bottomed cake tin for cheesecake. Crush biscuits and nuts and stir into melted margarine. Place in fridge.

10.25 Knead grated cheese into bap dough. Shape into four baps, cover and prove for 20 minutes to double.

10.35 Sieve the cottage cheese and beat in the yogurt. Dissolve gelatine. Whisk honey with egg yolks and stir this and the gelatine into the cheese mixture. Whisk egg whites until stiff and fold in. Pour mixture onto base and chill. At **10.50** bake baps.

11.10 Boil eggs for bagnat filling and pâté garnish. Make olive pâté. Pit olives, then blend until smooth with oil, garlic and seasoning. Smooth into pot and decorate.

12.00 Prepare chosen filling for bagnats and when loaves are cool, fill.

12.30 Wash lettuce and prepare herbs and cucumber for salad. If liked the dressing can be kept in jar until salad is to be served.

◀ **Pan Bagnat.**

BLACK OLIVE PÂTÉ

Black Olive Pâté
Serves 8
64 calories per portion
164 calories with 8 toast
triangles (four triangles to a
slice)

Imperial (Metric)
1 lb (450g) black olives, pitted
Sea salt, optional
1 tablespoonful olive oil
1 clove garlic, crushed
1 free-range egg, hard-boiled

American
4 cupsful black olives, pitted
Sea salt, optional
1 tablespoonful olive oil
1 clove garlic, crushed
1 free-range egg, hard-boiled

This recipe is unbelievably simple for such a delicious result. The only skill it demands is the patience to pit the olives.

Place all the ingredients in a liquidizer and blend until smooth. Pot and decorate the top with finely chopped hard-boiled egg.

Serve with crudités of complementary colours, such as white fennel, cauliflower and chicory leaves or use as a spread for hot wholemeal toast (no need to add butter) and eat with a side salad.

▲ Using a sharp knife pit the olives.

▲ Spread pâté on wholemeal toast.

PICNIC PIZZAS

Sauce:

Imperial (Metric)	American
1 large onion, finely chopped	1 large onion, finely chopped
2 cloves garlic, crushed	2 cloves garlic, crushed
1 dessertspoonful olive oil	2 teaspoonsful olive oil
1 teaspoonful oregano	1 teaspoonful oregano
1 red pepper, finely chopped	1 red pepper, finely chopped
15 oz (425g) fresh or tinned tomatoes	15 ounces fresh or canned tomatoes
Sea salt	Sea salt
Freshly ground black pepper	Freshly ground black pepper

Sauté the onion and garlic in the oil for two minutes. Stir in the oregano, red pepper and the tomatoes. Bring to the boil, reduce heat and simmer for 20 minutes, stirring occasionally until thick and pulpy. Season.

Dough:

Imperial (Metric)	American
1 lb (450g) wholemeal flour	4 cupsful wholewheat flour
1 oz (25g) soft vegetable margarine	¼ cupful soft vegetable margarine
1 teaspoonful sea salt	1 teaspoonful sea salt
1 oz (25g) fresh yeast	2½ tablespoonsful fresh yeast
1 teaspoonful honey	1 teaspoonful honey
25mg vitamin C tablet, crushed	25mg vitamin C tablet, crushed
½ pint (300ml) tepid water	2½ cupsful tepid water

Topping:

Imperial (Metric)	American
4 oz (100g) mushrooms, sliced	1½ cupsful sliced mushrooms
4 oz (100g) sweetcorn kernels	¾ cupful sweetcorn kernels
1 green pepper, sliced	1 green pepper, sliced

While the sauce is simmering prepare the dough. Rub the margarine into the flour and salt. Crumble the yeast with the honey and vitamin C tablet into the tepid water. Stir well and pour onto the flour. Mix to a soft dough. Turn out onto a lightly floured surface and knead for ten minutes until smooth. Cover and leave to rest for ten minutes.

When dough has rested roll out to ¼-inch (½cm) thick and using a three-inch (7cm) round cutter, cut out rounds. Place on a lightly greased baking tray and spoon a little tomato sauce onto each. Top with some mushrooms, sweetcorn and strips of pepper. Leave to prove in a warm place for ten minutes then bake at 425°F/232°C (Gas Mark 7) for 15 minutes.

● Additional topping suggestions: black olives, flakes of tuna fish, anchovies, Mozzarella or Edam cheese cut into fine slices, rings of courgette (zucchini).

▲ Knead pizza dough until smooth using the heel of the hand.

▲ Top each pizza with tomato sauce and prepared vegetables.

Picnic Pizzas
Makes 8 individual pizzas
250 calories per pizza

PAN BAGNAT

The flavour of Provence in a delicious wholemeal loaf. For best results make home-made bread. Two pounds (900g) of flour will make two super-size bagnats to feed four (see page 44, Menu 4). To fill one bagnat for two people use:

Imperial (Metric)	American
1½ oz (40g) anchovy fillets	¼ cupful anchovy fillets
2 oz (50g) black olives	½ cupful black olives
½ crisp lettuce heart	½ crisp lettuce heart
2 ripe tomatoes	2 ripe tomatoes
1 free-range egg, hard-boiled	1 free-range egg, hard-boiled
½ red pepper, de-seeded and sliced	½ red pepper, de-seeded and sliced
½ small onion, sliced	½ small onion, sliced

Drain the can of anchovies, using the oil, if liked, to 'butter' the bread. Drain the olives.

Finely shred the lettuce with a sharp knife and place half on the base of the bread. Top with slices of tomato, egg, pepper, onion, anchovies and olives. Top with rest of lettuce and the top half of the bread.

HUMMUS STICK

Use the same delicious bread, but try a vegetarian filling using Hummus (page 41, Menu 4). To fill one loaf which will serve two people use:

Imperial (Metric)	American
5 oz (150g) hummus	1¼ cupsful hummus
½ crisp lettuce heart	½ crisp lettuce heart
2 ripe tomatoes	2 ripe tomatoes
1 free-range hard-boiled egg	1 free-range hard-boiled egg
½ red or green pepper de-seeded and sliced	½ red or green pepper de-seeded and sliced

'Butter' the two halves of the loaf with the hummus. Place a layer of finely shredded lettuce on top. Arrange layers of other ingredients on top of lettuce.

▲ You can vary the fillings of baps and rolls to suit your own tastes.

CHEESE BAP

Add 2 ounces (50g) grated mature Cheddar cheese to each 1 pound (450g) bread dough. Add the cheese by kneading it into the dough. Shape dough into four baps and glaze with beaten free-range egg. Place on baking tray. Cover with clean teatowel (to prevent crust forming) and leave in warm place until doubled in size. Bake at 425°F/218°C (Gas Mark 7) for 20 minutes. Allow to cool before filling with mustard and cress.

Sandwich Specials
560 calories per Pan Bagnat,
Serves 2
400 calories per Hummus Stick,
Serves 2
130 calories per Cheese and
Cress Bap

GREEN SALAD

Imperial (Metric)
2 lettuce
½ cucumber
1 tablespoonful lemon juice
1 tablespoonful white wine vinegar
6 tablespoonsful olive oil
Sea salt
Freshly ground black pepper
1 tablespoonful freshly chopped
    herbs of choice

American
2 lettuce
½ cucumber
1 tablespoonful lemon juice
1 tablespoonful white wine vinegar
6 tablespoonsful olive oil
Sea salt
Freshly ground black pepper
1 tablespoonful freshly chopped
    herbs of choice

Discard any tough outer leaves from lettuce. Carefully remove remaining leaves from stem and wash under cold tap. Shake dry. Thinly slice the cucumber and place with lettuce in salad bowl. Combine the remaining ingredients in a screw-top jar and shake vigorously. Pour over lettuce and cucumber and toss together.

LIGHT LEMON CHEESECAKE

> **Light Lemon Cheesecake**
> **Serves 8**
> **239 calories per portion**

Biscuit base:

Imperial (Metric)
6 oz (175g) digestive wholemeal
    biscuits
2 oz (50g) soft vegetable margarine
2 oz (50g) crushed walnuts

American
6 ounces Graham crackers
¼ cupful soft vegetable margarine
½ cupful crushed English walnuts

Lightly oil an 8½-inch (22cm) springform, loose-bottomed cake tin. Place margarine in saucepan and melt over a low heat. Crush biscuits to fine crumbs by placing in large mixing bowl and pulverizing with pestle. Crush walnuts in pestle and mortar. Mix together crumbs, nuts and margarine and press into the base of the prepared tin. Place in fridge to set.

▲ Pour the whisked cheesecake
filling onto the biscuit base.

▲ Decorate with piped soft
cheese, lemon, chopped nuts.

Cheesecake filling:

Imperial (Metric)	American
12 oz (325g) cottage cheese	1½ cupsful cottage cheese
5 fl oz (150ml) thick set natural yogurt	⅔ cupful thick set natural yogurt
½ oz (12g) gelatine or agar agar	1 tablespoonful gelatine or agar agar
2 tablespoonsful water	2 tablespoonsful water
1 tablespoonful lemon juice	1 tablespoonful lemon juice
2 free-range eggs, separated	2 free-range eggs, separated
1 tablespoonful clear honey	1 tablespoonful clear honey
Grated rind of lemon	Grated rind of lemon

Press cottage cheese through sieve and mix with yogurt. Place gelatine or agar agar in saucepan with water and lemon juice and heat, stirring continuously, until dissolved. Remove from heat and allow to cool.

Place egg yolks in mixing bowl and whisk with honey until thick, pale and ropey. Stir gelatine mixture and honey mixture into the cheese. Add grated lemon rind. Whisk egg whites until they form stiff peaks and fold into mixture with a metal spoon. Pour on top of base and return to fridge to chill for two hours before serving.

Decorate with small slices of lemon and chopped walnuts and piped noisettes of soft curd cheese or whipped cream.

Nutritional Notes — Menu 9

Pack up a healthy, wholefood picnic by following our ideas for turning outdoor meals into something more than sandwiches.

We've turned to the Mediterranean for inspiration for summer snacks. Black Olive Pâté simply combines black olives with garlic to make a tasty starter, spread on toast, crackers or serve with raw vegetable crudités. Olives are high in fibre and supply small amounts of B vitamins and minerals too. They also contain around 11 per cent fat. Olives are pressed to produce olive oil, one of the more healthy oils, with a high concentration of unsaturated and polyunsaturated fatty acids.

Black olives could also be used to decorate our Picnic Pizzas. Made from the speedy vitamin C bread recipe, picnic pizzas are spread with a home-made tomato sauce and then finally decorated with your choice from a selection of quick cooking vegetables — like sweetcorn kernels, strips of peppers, mushrooms or rings of courgettes. Mozzarella cheese is traditionally used to give a fine covering of melted cheese but Edam makes a lower calorie and cheaper alternative. Or omit cheese altogether if you prefer.

Anchovies or tuna fish could also be added to pizzas and to our wholemeal Pan Bagnats. Again made with vitamin C bread recipe, pan bagnats, a traditional snack from Provence can be filled with salad ingredients and to balance the protein either fish, hard-boiled free-range eggs or hummus.

Another variation on a basic bread dough is a cheese bap. Inspired by Cranks' famous cheese baps ours are made by mixing grated cheese into a basic wholemeal dough before shaping, proving and baking. Filled with cress they make a colourful addition to any lunch box, especially suitable for children. Salads are easy to transport — wash ingredients before leaving home but toss in dressing just as you're ready to eat to maintain crispness.

Complete your meal with a light tangy cheesecake. Most cheesecake recipes depend on double cream and cream cheese to give a solid texture and rich flavour. But laden with fat recipes like these are high in calories and can be cloying. We have substituted sieved cottage cheese for cream cheese, and yogurt for double cream to give a lower calorie version. A little honey sweetens the mixture, while gelatine or agar agar is used to set the mixture. Finally stiffly whisked egg whites give a refreshing lightness.

Our biscuit base leaves out the sugar that many recipes include and adds crushed walnuts to give extra fibre and flavour. Choose wholemeal biscuits for less sweetness but a good texture. Once the cheesecake is set it can be cut into wedges before you pack your picnic — otherwise remember to take a good knife with you. Pack up bottled water or cartons of fresh fruit juice to complete the meal.

Fresh Fruit Salad. ➤

Menu 10

Stuffed Courgettes
Poached Salmon
Oatcakes
Fresh Fruit Salad

Menu 10
Time plan

USE this time plan as a guide for making all, or one, of these dishes. If you plan to eat earlier or later simply put the clock back or forward on our time plan.

5.45 Start preparing court bouillon. Peel and chop vegetables and place in pan with white wine and water and bring to the boil. Simmer for 20 minutes cool and strain just before using.

6.00 Light oven 375°F/190°C (Gas Mark 5). Mix oatmeal, flour, baking powder together and stir in melted margarine and sufficient boiling water to mix to a dough. Roll out into a rectangle and cut into triangular oatcakes. Bake 10-15 minutes.

6.30 Halve courgettes (zucchini), scoop out flesh and chop finely. Prepare the filling and stuff the shells. Set aside.

7.00 Start preparing syrup and fruit for fruit salad, leaving apples, pears and bananas till last.

7.10 Bake courgettes (zucchini).

7.20 Place salmon steaks in flat dish and cover with strained court bouillon. Bake 15-20 minutes. Put new potatoes on to cook.

7.30 Steam or lightly boil beans and peas. Serve courgettes (zucchini).

STUFFED COURGETTES

> **Stuffed Courgettes**
> **Serves 4**
> **115 calories per portion.**

Imperial (Metric)
4 small or 2 large courgettes
1 large onion
2 cloves garlic
1 tablespoonful olive oil
2 tomatoes, skinned and chopped
1½ oz (40g) wholemeal
   breadcrumbs
1 tablespoonful chopped parsley
1 teaspoonful dried oregano
Freshly ground black pepper
2 oz (50g) pine kernels
2 tablespoonsful cold water

American
4 small or 2 large zucchini
1 large onion
2 cloves garlic
1 tablespoonful olive oil
2 tomatoes, skinned and chopped
¾ cupful wholewheat breadcrumbs
1 tablespoonful chopped parsley
1 teaspoonful dried oregano
Freshly ground black pepper
½ cupful pine kernels
2 tablespoonsful cold water

Cut courgettes (zucchini) in half lengthwise. Scoop out flesh and chop finely. Finely chop the onion and crush the garlic. *Sauté* together in the oil for two minutes. Stir into the onion mixture the chopped tomatoes, courgette (zucchini) flesh, breadcrumbs, herbs, seasoning and pine kernels. Continue cooking over a low heat for a further two minutes. Place shells in a shallow ovenproof dish. Divide filling between the shells and press in firmly. Spoon the water in base of dish. Place in a pre-heated oven 400°F/204°C (Gas Mark 6) for 15-20 minutes until topping has browned slightly.

COURT BOUILLON

Imperial (Metric)	**American**
2 carrots	2 carrots
1 onion	1 onion
2 sticks celery	2 stalks celery
2 shallots	2 shallots
1 bay leaf	1 bay leaf
3 parsley stalks	3 parsley stalks
2 sprigs thyme	2 sprigs thyme
Juice of half a lemon	Juice of half a lemon
½ pint (300ml) dry white wine	1⅔ cupsful dry white wine
1½ pints (1 litre) water	3¾ cupsful water
6 black peppercorns	6 black peppercorns

Peel and finely chop carrots, onion, celery and shallots. Place all ingredients in a large saucepan. Cover and bring to the boil. Lower heat and simmer for 20 minutes. Remove from heat and allow to cool. Strain before use.

Dice the onion and prepare other vegetables for the court bouillon.▼

Pour strained court bouillon over the salmon and add a twist of pepper.▼

Court bouillon is a simple stock to make. It will take only 40 minutes before it is ready for use and it illustrates the benefits of taking time to make home-made stocks and sauces. No matter how good a stock cube, and there are some good vegetable bouillon cubes available in health food shops, they cannot match the fine flavour of real stock, particularly in a recipe as subtle and delicate as Poached Salmon.

> **Poached Salmon**
> **Serves 4**
> **180 calories per 4 oz (100g)**
>   **salmon steak**
> **180 calories for the Court**
>   **Bouillon**

POACHED SALMON

Imperial (Metric)
4 × 4-6 oz (100-175g) salmon steaks
Court bouillon to cover, about 1 pint
   (600ml), depending on size of
   ovenproof dish

American
4 × 4-6 ounce salmon steaks
Court bouillon to cover, about 2½
   cupsful, depending on size of
   ovenproof dish

Set oven to 350°F/177°C (Gas Mark 4). Wash salmon steaks and place in a flat ovenproof dish. Cover with court bouillon and place in centre of oven. Bake for 15-20 minutes.

★   ★   ★

Salmon is an expensive fish, but if used as a main course for a dinner it is no more expensive than an equivalent meat main course. Halibut and turbot are slightly cheaper and very nice.

   For more economical fishes to poach, choose cod or haddock steaks. Or roll fillets of flat fish, such as sole and whiting, with chopped onion inside the rolls. Round fish such as mackerel and herring (both very economical) can also be filled and rolled and poached.

OATCAKES

Imperial (Metric)	American
8 oz (225g) medium oatmeal	2 cupsful medium oatmeal
2 oz (50g) wholemeal flour	½ cupful wholewheat flour
1 teaspoonful baking powder	1 teaspoonful baking soda
2 oz (50g) soft vegetable margarine	¼ cupful soft vegetable margarine
Boiling water to mix	Boiling water to mix

Pre-set oven to 375°F/190°C (Gas Mark 5). Mix oatmeal, flour and baking powder in a mixing bowl. Melt margarine in a saucepan and stir into dry ingredients. Gradually add enough boiling water to make a dough, being careful not to add too much. Turn onto a lightly floured surface and knead until dough is firm enough to roll out. Roll dough into a rectangle. Trim edges and cut into triangular oatcakes. Slip palette knife under oatcakes and carefully lift onto non-stick or lightly oiled baking tray. Sprinkle with a little oatmeal and bake for 10-15 minutes.

Oatcakes ▲
Makes 20 oatcakes, 66 calories per oatcake
200 calories per 2 ounces (50g) portion mature Cheddar,
165 calories for Brie, 150 calories for Edam, 230 calories for Blue Stilton

FRESH FRUIT SALAD

Fresh Fruit Salad
Serves 4
115 calories per portion

Imperial (Metric)
1 teaspoonful honey
3 tablespoonsful cold water
1 honeydew melon, halved
2 oranges
½ small pineapple
Small bunch white grapes
Small bunch black grapes
8 oz (225g) plums
1 kiwifruit
8 oz (225g) red skinned apples
Juice of 2 lemons
2 firm eating pears
1 banana

American
1 teaspoonful honey
3 tablespoonsful cold water
1 honeydew melon, halved
2 oranges
½ small pineapple
Small bunch white grapes
Small bunch black grapes
8 ounces plums
1 kiwifruit
8 ounces red skinned apples
Juice of 2 lemons
2 firm eating pears
1 banana

Place honey and water in small pan and heat gently until honey is thoroughly mixed in. Cool. Cut melon in half and using a melon baller cut out balls. Peel the oranges and cut into fine horizontal slices. Cut pineapple into rings, then remove peel. Cut into chunks. Wash grapes well. Half and remove pips. Wash plums, cut in half and remove stones. Peel and cut kiwifruit into fine slices. Cut apples into quarters and remove core. Slice thinly and place in lemon juice to stop browning. Peel pears, remove core and cut into small chunks and mix with the apples and lemon juice, peel and slice the bananas and mix with the juice also.

If liked, mix all prepared fruit together with the syrup. Alternatively arrange in layers for a more dramatic effect. Vary the type of fruit you use according to availability.

Nutritional Notes — Menu 10

Serve fresh salmon at any dinner party and your guests will feel that they are being spoilt. It's true fresh salmon is expensive, but it is no more so than expensive cuts of meat or a joint, and the flavour is so much nicer.

Salmon is also delicious and far more easily digested than meat, so your guests will thank you for not leaving them with that, 'Very nice, but far too rich' feeling. We have poached the Scotch salmon steaks in a home-made court bouillon stock. This enhances the true colour and flavour of the fish and does not mask it like heavy *beurre blanc* and other traditional creamy sauces.

Fish poached in stock also has the benefit of far fewer calories than fish grilled with butter or fried; compare 22 calories per ¼ pint (150ml) of court bouillon with 899 calories for the same amount of vegetable oil.

Serve the salmon with boiled new potatoes and fresh runner beans or French beans and for extra fibre add a serving of fresh garden peas, because fish, like meat, is fibreless. However it does have the advantage of containing unsaturated fatty acids.

Slightly oily fish like salmon is best for poaching but other, cheaper fish that can be cut into steaks, such as cod and haddock, can be poached. Fish steaks are usually used for poaching but rolled fillets (held together with a wooden cocktail stick) of sole, brill, or whiting can also be used.

The accent is on freshness in this summer menu. Courgettes (zucchini) will be in full production in the garden, and a good crop will mean you can be extravagant and choose baby courgettes for stuffing to make a delicious starter.

Remember to cook the vegetables only to *al dente* texture; that is offering some resistance when bitten, not soggy and overcooked, and you will retain colour, flavour, texture and those important vitamins and minerals from garden-fresh produce.

Summer nights and days can be sultry which is why our menu is so refreshing. A cooling fresh fruit salad is a delightful way to finish a meal. Make it at the last minute just before the guests arrive and put it in the fridge to chill before serving. Don't let it get too cold or the flavour of the fruit will be lost.

Never spoil a fresh fruit salad by adding anything from a can. Better to have fewer varieties and keep them fresh. A fruit salad will tempt people more than a bowl of fresh fruit because they can have something of everything and not slice their way through a whole apple, pear, mango or whatever.

Don't feel you have to offer heavy cream with fruit salad. It ruins the flavour and appearance as it curdles in the bowl with the fruit juice. Keep it simple.

For a very special occasion a fourth course of cheese and biscuits could be served, especially if you have stuck to nice small portions. This low-fat meal which is low in calories and light in texture will still leave room for cheese and biscuits.

Home-made oatcakes are far nicer than the shop-bought cheese biscuits made from white flour with a liberal sprinkling of additives.

Oatcakes are simple to make and can be made the day before and stored in an airtight tin when completely cold. Oatmeal will add fibre to the meal and oats are now known to have a very special type of fibre (different from wheat bran fibre) whose gummy consistency is able to help lower the amount of harmful cholesterol found in the bloodstream and so be protective against heart disease.

Eating about 2 ounces (50g) of oats a day is thought to help control the amount of fats in the blood and help lower high blood pressure.

Remember that cheese is a high-fat food so do not eat too much at the end of the meal — just enough to enjoy with the crunchy, tasty oatcakes.

Menu 11

Ratatouille
Brazil Ring Bake
Apple Gateau
Tofu Burgers (alternative main course)

Menu 11
Time plan

USE this time plan as a guide for making all, or one, of these dishes. If you plan to eat earlier or later simply put the clock back or forward on our time plan.

5.15 Light oven 375°F/190°C (Gas Mark 5). Lightly oil and line cake tin. Whisk eggs and honey together over low heat. Fold in flour and melted margarine. Pour into tin and bake 25-30 minutes.

5.45 Scrub the aubergine (eggplant) and slice thinly. Plunge into boiling water and cook for two minutes. Drain. Prepare courgettes (zucchini), tomatoes, peppers, onions and garlic. Cook in olive oil, covered, for 45 minutes. Either chill or set aside and then reheat just before serving.

6.00 Wash, core and slice the apples. Cook gently to a pulp. Sieve and cool.

6.30 Light oven 400°F/204°C (Gas Mark 6). Grind the nuts and mix with breadcrumbs, onions, pepper, celery and sage. Add tomato *purée*, beaten egg and stock. Press into oiled ring mould and bake for 40 minutes.

7.00 Mix apple *purée* with soft cheese for gateau. Cut gateau into three and sandwich together with the apple mixture and spread a fine layer on top of cake. Thinly slice some apples and dip in lemon juice to decorate top, with nuts.

7.20 Wash watercress and if liked put some scrubbed potatoes on to cook to serve with the Brazil Ring Bake. Reheat ratatouille if liked.

7.30 Serve ratatouille.

Ratatouille
Serves 4
160 calories per portion

◄ **Brazil Ring Bake.**

Ratatouille makes a dish rich in colour, vitamins and fibre. ►

RATATOUILLE

Imperial (Metric)	American
1 aubergine	1 eggplant
2 courgettes	2 zucchini
2 tomatoes	2 tomatoes
1 green pepper	1 green pepper
1 red pepper	1 red pepper
1 onion	1 onion
1 clove garlic	1 clove garlic
4 tablespoonsful olive oil	4 tablespoonsful olive oil
Freshly ground black pepper	Freshly ground black pepper

Scrub the aubergine (eggplant) and slice thinly. Plunge into boiling water and cook for two minutes. Drain. Scrub and slice the courgettes (zucchini). Chop the washed tomatoes. Wash and de-seed the peppers. Cut into rings. Peel and slice the onion. Peel the garlic clove and crush. Place olive oil in heavy-based saucepan with a well-fitting lid. Add the vegetables and cover. Cook over a low heat for 45 minutes, stirring several times to ensure vegetables are cooked evenly. Season with freshly ground black pepper about ten minutes from end of cooking. Equally good served hot or cold as a salad.

 N.B. Pre-cooking the aubergine a little will prevent it soaking up all the oil and avoid the temptation to add more oil (and more calories).

BRAZIL RING BAKE

Imperial (Metric)	**American**
6 oz (175g) shelled Brazil nuts	1 ¼ cupsful shelled Brazil nuts
6 oz (175g) wholemeal breadcrumbs	3 cupsful wholewheat breadcrumbs
1 large onion	1 large onion
1 green pepper	1 green pepper
2 sticks celery	2 stalks celery
1 dessertspoonful chopped fresh sage or ½ teaspoonful dried sage	2 teaspoonsful finely chopped fresh sage or ½ teaspoonful dried sage
2 tablespoonsful tomato purée	2 tablespoonsful tomato paste
1 beaten free-range egg	1 beaten free-range egg
3 fl oz (90ml) vegetable stock	⅓ cupful vegetable stock
Sea salt	Sea salt
Freshly ground black pepper	Freshly ground black pepper

Grind the nuts in a liquidizer or chop very finely. Mix with the breadcrumbs. Finely chop the onion and pepper and celery. Add to the nut mixture with the sage. Mix in thoroughly. Stir in the tomato *purée*, beaten egg and stock. Season lightly and mix in thoroughly. Lightly oil an eight-inch (20cm) ring mould. Place mixture in ring and press down firmly. Place in a pre-heated oven, 400°F/204°C (Gas Mark 6) and cook for 40 minutes. Cool slightly before removing from ring.

TOFU BURGERS

Imperial (Metric)	American
3 oz (75g) long-grain brown rice, cooked and cooled	⅓ cupful long-grain brown rice, cooked and cooled
2 oz (50g) carrot, grated	⅓ cupful grated carrot
2 oz (50g) mushroom, finely chopped	¾ cupful finely chopped mushrooms
2 oz (50g) onion, finely chopped	⅓ cupful finely chopped onion
10 oz (275g) tofu	1⅔ cupsful tofu
½ teaspoonful sage	½ teaspoonful sage
1½ teaspoonsful soy sauce	1½ teaspoonsful soy sauce
Freshly ground black pepper	Freshly ground black pepper
Sea salt	Sea salt
Wholemeal breadcrumbs	Wholewheat breadcrumbs
Vegetable oil to cook	Vegetable oil to cook

Mix the cooked rice with the grated carrot, chopped mushrooms and onion. Drain the tofu and place in a clean cloth. Gently squeeze out excess moisture. Remove from cloth and crumble into rice mixture stirring in thoroughly. Add the sage, soy sauce and seasoning. Divide the mixture into six. Shape each into a flat burger and coat in breadcrumbs. Place in refrigerator for an hour to firm up. Place enough vegetable oil in frying pan to coat base and heat. Place tofu burgers in the oil and cook for four minutes each side until golden and crispy. Drain off fat and serve.

Brazil Ring Bake **Serves 6** **260 calories per portion**	**Tofu Burgers** **Makes 6** **118 calories per burger**

◄◄ Chop vegetables for a coarse textured roast or liquidize for a smooth result.

◄ Place prepared roast mixture in savarin ring ready for baking.

APPLE GATEAU

Apple Gateau
Serves 8
280 calories per portion

Imperial (Metric)
1½ oz (40g) unsalted butter or soft
   vegetable margarine
3 oz (75g) wholemeal flour
2 oz (50g) honey
3 free-range eggs

Filling and topping:

Imperial (Metric)
1 lb (450g) apples
4 oz (100g) low-fat white cheese
2 oz (50g) toasted almond flakes

American
4 tablespoonsful unsalted butter or
   soft vegetable margarine
¾ cupful wholewheat flour
2 tablespoonsful honey
3 free-range eggs

American
1 pound apples
½ cupful low-fat white cheese
½ cupful toasted almond slivers

▲ Carefully slice the cooled
sponge in two or three layers
with a palette knife.

▲ Decorate the gateau with
sliced fresh apple and toasted
flaked almonds.

Pre-set oven to 375°F/190°C (Gas Mark 5). Grease and line an eight-inch cake tin with greased greaseproof paper. Place fat in saucepan and melt over a low heat. Remove from heat. Sieve flour into a mixing bowl and stand in a warm place. Place eggs and honey in the top half of a double boiler or in a bowl standing in a pan of hot water and whisk until thick, pale and ropey. Fold the sieved flour into the egg mixture using a metal spoon. Add the melted fat by pouring down the side of the mixing bowl and fold in with the metal spoon. Pour into prepared cake tin and bake until firm and set — about 25-30 minutes. Allow to cool. While the sponge is cooking wash and core the apples. Slice into a saucepan with a few tablespoonsful of water and cook covered over a low heat until pulped; about 15 minutes. Remove from heat, sieve and allow to cool before stirring in the cheese.

When the sponge is cold cut carefully into three layers using a palette knife. Sandwich together with apple mixture and put a layer on top and sides of finished gateau. Press toasted almonds onto sides of gateau and use any extra *purée* to pipe noisettes on top.

Nutritional Notes — Menu 11

Nut cutlets have been the butt of many jokes about vegetarian eating. Nut roasts are often treated in a similar vein and having tried some rather dry varieties it is not surprising.

However, our nut roast has a sophistication of colour and presentation that at once shows how delicious a nut roast can be. Getting away from the traditional loaf tin shape turns the nut roast into a party dish and the tomato *purée* used in the paste mixture gives it a subtle pink shade that would make any critic blush with shame.

For anyone who wants to place more emphasis on vegetable sources of protein it is important to have a useful supply of nut recipes because they are an excellent source of protein. This recipe contains breadcrumbs which ensures all the amino acids necessary for the body to make protein are present. Combining two of the three basic vegetable protein groups (nuts, pulses or cereal grains) at the main protein meal of the day will ensure the protein is complete.

Nuts are high in fibre, so they have another advantage over animal sources of protein which are fibreless, but nuts are also high in fat so they should be used sparingly. However, the oil they contain is unsaturated so this is an advantage. Few recipes use Brazil nuts, which is a shame as they have a unique flavour and they are readily available fresh in the shell.

It is always best to buy unshelled nuts because the process of shelling exposes the kernel to oxygen and starts off the process of deterioration which can turn the oils rancid. Don't keep too long and store in cool, dry conditions.

Serving a nut roast with watercress makes a good colour complement and also gives a valuable source of vitamin C and iron, both of which should be eaten together to make the iron more easily absorbed by the body. Vegetarians are at particular risk of being short of iron because one of the best sources is meat.

Another useful source of vegetable protein is tofu. This soyabean curd has been used as a staple food for many years in the Far East (see page 72, Menu 7), but it does not have the fibre content of nuts. However it is almost fat-free and so is low in calories.

Tofu comes from soyabeans so needs balancing with either a nut or grain to complete the protein. Cooked brown rice is used in the tofu burgers to balance the protein and finely chopped or grated vegetables and soy sauce and sage add colour and flavour. Remember not to deep fry, instead add a little oil to a shallow frying pan and cook briskly to give a crunchy coating of breadcrumbs. Less oil is absorbed, especially if it is heated before adding the burgers.

Apple gateau is an excellent way to use the new season's apples available in September and October. By making the gateau with a whisked sponge recipe you will run less risk of having a 'flop' using wholemeal flour. This method is also low in fat and therefore low in calories.

Making an apple *purée* and mixing it with a low-fat soft white cheese gives a flavour that is tangy without being sharp and one that contrasts with the honey flavour of the sponge gateau.

▲ **Tofu Burgers make an informal supper dish.**

Menu 12

Prawns on Asparagus
Barley Casserole with Parsley Dumplings
Blackberry Charlotte
Carob Cake

Menu 12
Time plan

USE this time plan as a guide for making all, or one, of these dishes. If you plan to eat earlier or later simply put the clock back or forward on our time plan.

5.45 Cook breadcrumbs for Blackberry Charlotte over a low heat. Cool and stir in the sugar and cinnamon. Wash blackberries and pick over. Cook gently for a couple of minutes to bring out the juice. Place half the crumbs in base of glass dish, top with blackberries and then finish with crumbs. Chill.

6.10 If using oven to cook casserole light oven 350°F/177°C (Gas Mark 4). Cook onions with carrots for five minutes then add flour and stock gradually bringing to the boil. Add mushrooms, barley and season. Cook for one hour.

6.25 If serving baked potatoes, clean four medium sized potatoes and prick with fork. Bake.

7.00 Mix dumplings, shape and place in top of casserole.

7.10 Shell prawns, reserving few for garnish. *Purée* asparagus (first steamed if using fresh) with stock, pepper, butter and flour. Cook over a low heat bringing mixture to boil. Simmer till thick. While cooking warm scallop dishes. Plunge prawns in boiling water and cook two minutes. Drain. Arrange asparagus in dishes, top with prawns and garnish. Serve immediately.

◄ **Barley Casserole with Parsley Dumplings.**

Prawns contrast well in colour and texture with asparagus *purée.* ►

PRAWNS ON ASPARAGUS

| Prawns on Asparagus |
| Serves 4 |
| 96 calories per portion |

Imperial (Metric)
3 oz (75g) shelled prawns or
* 6 oz (175g) unshelled prawns*
1 lb (450g) fresh asparagus or
* 10 oz (275g) can*
¼ pint (150ml) turkey, chicken or
* vegetable stock*
Freshly ground black pepper
1 tablespoonful unsalted butter
1 tablespoonful wholemeal flour
1 pint (600ml) boiling water
1 tablespoonful freshly chopped
* chives*

American
3 ounces shelled prawns or
* 6 ounces unshelled prawns*
1 pound fresh asparagus or
* 1 medium can*
⅔ cupful turkey, chicken or
* vegetable stock*
Freshly ground black pepper
1 tablespoonful unsalted butter
1 tablespoonful wholewheat flour
2½ cupsful boiling water
1 tablespoonful freshly chopped
* chives*

Shell the prawns, reserving four in shells for garnish. If using fresh asparagus prepare as for Spring Vegetable Salad (page 57, Menu 6). If using canned, drain. Reserve four tips for decoration. Place chopped asparagus, stock, pepper, butter and flour in liquidizer and blend until smooth. Transfer to a heavy-based saucepan and stir continuously over a low heat until the mixture comes to the boil. Lower heat and simmer to form a thick *purée*. Place four well-scrubbed scallop shells or ceramic shell dishes under a grill to warm. Plunge the prawns into the boiling water. Cover and cook for two to three minutes until heated through. Spoon the *purée* onto the serving dishes and drain the prawns. Arrange prawns on top of each dish of asparagus *purée*. Garnish with unshelled prawns, chives and asparagus tips and serve immediately.

BARLEY CASSEROLE

Imperial (Metric)	American
8 oz (225g) pot or Scotch barley	1 cupful pot barley
2 carrots, scrubbed and diced	2 carrots, scrubbed and diced
2 onions, peeled and diced	2 onions, peeled and diced
1 tablespoonful vegetable oil	1 tablespoonful vegetable oil
1 tablespoonful wholemeal flour	1 tablespoonful wholewheat flour
1½ pints (750ml) vegetable stock or	3¾ cupsful vegetable stock or
1 vegetable bouillon cube	1 vegetable bouillon cube and
and 1½ pints (750ml) water	3¾ cupsful water
1 teaspoonful yeast extract	1 teaspoonful yeast extract
1 teaspoonful readymade	1 teaspoonful readymade
stoneground mustard	stoneground mustard
Freshly ground black pepper	Freshly ground black pepper
8 oz (225g) mushrooms, sliced	3 cupsful sliced mushrooms

Place carrots and onions in heavy-based saucepan or casserole with oil. Cover and sweat for five minutes. Stir in the flour to coat vegetables evenly. Gradually add the stock, stirring all the time, and bring to the boil. Add seasoning, mushrooms and barley. Stir well and cover. Cook over a low heat for 1 hour either on top of the stove or transfer to a moderate oven, 350°F/177°C (Gas Mark 4). After 40 minutes, add dumplings.

Prepare vegetables for casserole. Pressure cook if liked. ➤

Shape dumplings into four rounds and place in casserole for last 20 minutes. ▼

Casserole with Parsley Dumplings
Serves 4
244 per casserole portion
145 per dumpling

PARSLEY DUMPLINGS

Imperial (Metric)
4 oz (100g) wholemeal flour
1½ teaspoonsful baking powder
1½ oz (40g) soft vegetable
  margarine
1 tablespoonful chopped parsley
Freshly ground black pepper
Cold water to mix

American
1 cupful wholewheat flour
1½ teaspoonsful baking soda
4 tablespoonsful soft vegetable
  margarine
1 tablespoonful chopped parsley
Freshly ground black pepper
Cold water to mix

Sieve flour and baking powder into mixing bowl. Rub in fat until mixture resembles breadcrumbs in consistency. Stir in parsley and pepper. Mix to a soft dough with cold water. Form into four balls or roll out and cut into four thick scone shapes with cutters.

BLACKBERRY CHARLOTTE

Imperial (Metric)	American
2 oz (50g) soft vegetable margarine or unsalted butter	¼ cupful soft vegetable margarine or unsalted butter
6 oz (175g) wholemeal breadcrumbs	3 cupsful wholewheat breadcrumbs
1 oz (25g) Demerara sugar	2 tablespoonsful Demerara sugar
½ teaspoonful ground cinnamon	½ teaspoonful ground cinnamon
1 lb (450g) blackberries	4 cupsful blackberries

Melt margarine or butter in large saucepan. Stir in the breadcrumbs and cook over a low heat in the fat until they turn golden brown and crispy. Remove from heat and cool. Stir in the sugar and cinnamon. Wash and pick over blackberries. Place in a pan and cook gently for a couple of minutes to bring out juice. Spoon juice off and set blackberries aside. Place half the breadcrumbs in the base of a glass dish. Spoon blackberries on top. Finish with a layer of crumbs. Chill.

Blackberry Charlotte
Serves 4
240 calories per portion

Lightly cook blackberries and pour over cooked breadcrumbs. ▼

Place second layer of bread- crumbs on top of blackberries. ▼

CAROB CAKE

Carob Cake
Serves 10
270 calories per slice

Imperial (Metric)
4 oz (100g) wholemeal flour
2 oz (50g) carob powder
2 teaspoonsful baking powder
6 oz (175g) soft vegetable margarine
4 oz (100g) Muscovado sugar
2 tablespoonsful clear honey
3 free-range eggs
2 tablespoonsful milk to mix

American
1 cupful wholewheat flour
½ cupful carob powder
2 teaspoonsful baking soda
¾ cupful soft vegetable margarine
⅔ cupful Muscovado sugar
2 tablespoonsful clear honey
3 free-range eggs
2 tablespoonsful milk to mix

Filling:

Imperial (Metric)
4 oz (100g) low-fat soft cheese
Juice of half a lemon
1 banana

American
½ cupful low-fat soft cheese
Juice of half a lemon
1 banana

Topping:

Imperial (Metric)
1 carob bar
Knob of unsalted butter or soft
*   vegetable margarine*
A few walnut halves

American
1 carob bar
Knob of unsalted butter or soft
*   vegetable margarine*
A few English walnut halves

Grease two seven-inch (18cm) cake tins. Sieve together flour, carob and baking powder. Dust the bran remaining in sieve inside the two cake tins. Cream together the margarine, sugar and honey until fluffy. Beat in one egg at a time, beating well between each egg. Fold in the sieved flour and carob with a metal spoon. Stir in the milk to mix to a soft dropping consistency. Divide the mixture between the two tins and lightly smooth the top until level. Place in the centre of a pre-heated oven, 350°F/177°C (Gas Mark 4) for 35-40 minutes until the cakes are well risen and spring back when touched with a fingertip. Place tins on a wire tray to cool for a couple of minutes before turning out and leaving to cool completely.

Mix the soft cheese with lemon juice. Peel banana and chop finely. Mash with a fork into the soft cheese mixture, until thoroughly blended. Spread evenly on one cake.

Melt carob bar in a small ovenproof bowl over a pan of hot water. Add butter or margarine and beat together until smooth and glossy. Using a palette knife quickly spread over the top of second cake until quite smooth. Place walnut halves on top. When set place cake on top of other half.

▼ **An excellent cake for a special occasion.**

Nutritional Notes — Menu 12

Dumplings are something most people who change to a healthier way of eating think they will never taste again. Our recipe substitutes ordinary soft vegetable margarine for the traditional suet and by flavouring with fresh parsley brings back those memories of warming winter casseroles.

Wholemeal flour is another improvement on the traditional dumpling and they make a welcome change from potatoes (and yet more potatoes) in winter menus. Barley is a nutritious grain with valuable amounts of B vitamins, potassium, phosphorus and calcium.

When buying barley choose pot or Scotch barley. Pearl barley found in supermarkets has been polished and refined to lose much of its original fibre and nutrients.

The hedgerow fruits of autumn provide one of the few occasions when you can pick something for nothing. Blackberries are a good example and provided they are picked from bushes well away from main roads and therefore away from lead pollution and from sites that have not been sprayed with chemicals they are excellent nutritional value. High in vitamin C and dietary fibre (unless you sieve out the pips from blackberry *purées*) they are a good basis for desserts (fruit fool, mousse or ice-cream) or sauce.

Our Blackberry Charlotte uses wholemeal breadcrumbs and is a good use for any stale bread that you might have. It is another economical dish that is full of goodness.

Because of the low cost of the other courses you might feel able to splash out on some more extravagant ingredients for a rather special starter. Prawns are costly, but only a few are needed to garnish this dish. Eating prawns is very much a matter of personal taste, like other shellfish they are a good source of low-fat protein and minerals like potassium, calcium, phosphorus, and magnesium but they are also high in salt.

As this is the last menu in the course we could not let the opportunity pass without making a cake which we hope you will share and enjoy as much as we have enjoyed creating the course.

It will also prove that you can make excellent cakes using wholemeal flour and that the children's birthday cake need not be a thing of the past if you set out to improve the family's diet. By using carob, you can make a very acceptable 'chocolate' flavoured cake without the stimulants found in chocolate (caffeine and theobromine) or the large amounts of oxalic acid found in chocolate that can lead to spotty faces among older children, by blocking calcium absorption which is needed for zinc assimilation — vital for healthy skin.

Carob is also free from the added sugar of chocolate and is naturally sweeter and lower in calories. It also contains potassium, calcium, magnesium, iron and vitamins A, D and three B vitamins.

Try mashing a banana with some low-fat soft cheese for a cake filling rather than using whipped cream or sugary jam; it goes well with the carob flavour and is low-calorie too.

INDEX

JEAN CONIL'S CUISINE VÉGÉTARIENNE FRANCAISE

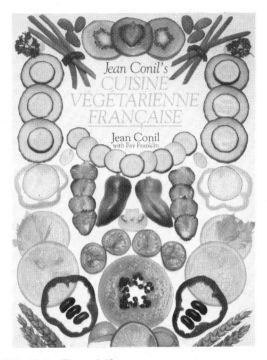

Jean Conil with Fay Franklin

The traditional cookery of France contains a wealth of delicious vegetarian dishes which are often overlooked by the world of *haute cuisine*. With the recent revolution in French cookery, there has been a move away from extravagant dishes swamped in rich sauces towards simpler, more natural flavours and textures, using fresh vegetables with variety and imagination. **Jean Conil,** President of the Society of Master Chefs, has drawn together these two concepts, along with the best of classic French cuisine, to create his own unique collection of the finest French vegetarian dishes, to satisfy any gourmet, delight vegetarians and wholefooders everywhere and show sceptical meat-eaters how much they have been missing out! Each recipe includes advice or special chef's tips and anecdotes gleaned from a lifetime in the finest restaurants of France and Britain.

COLIN SPENCER'S CORDON VERT

Dinner parties for every week of the year

Colin Spencer, Britain's foremost newspaper columnist on wholefood and vegetarian cooking, here presents luxurious wholefood meals which will delight both the gourmet vegetarian and the meat-eater alike, and prove conclusively that vegetarian food can not only rival the traditional meat-based dinner, but come out ahead and with flying colours. Includes wine and liquer suggestions to perfectly complement the different courses of every meal, with the emphasis squarely on luxury. Fine wines, rare cheeses, exotic fruit and vegetables; all give that special dinner its memorable character. Far from being extravagant or over indulgent, you will find they are perfect for turning a dinner party into an occasion to be remembered.

THE VERY BEST OF VEGETARIAN COOKING

Edited by Janet Hunt. It wasn't so long ago that vegetarians were regarded as an eccentric minority, and if not mocked then at least pitied for the way they must surely suffer at mealtimes. Now however all that is changing. Vegetarians exist in such large numbers that they can no longer be dismissed as a minority nor can they be ignored. Janet Hunt, the well known wholefood cookery writer, has here compiled an excellent collection of wholefood recipes — presented on high quality paper with many full-colour photographs — including the best of Indian curries, Italian dishes, salads, slimmers' meals, winter warmers, bread, rice dishes, desserts and many exciting new recipes. She creates a bonanza of imaginative gourmet eating, to titillate the palate and delight the eye.

EVELYN FINDLATER'S
NATURAL FOODS PRIMER

A Beginner's Guide to Choosing and Using Wholefoods

What ARE wholefoods? What IS fibre? Does it REALLY matter what I eat? How can I make the change-over and still eat tasty, filling foods? **Evelyn Findlater** — long-time devotee of vegetarian foods, health shop and cafe owner, cookery teacher and 'healthy school meals' supervisor, here answers all the questions you've ever wanted to ask about wholefoods but were too embarrassed to ask. A fascinating and appetizing introduction to the world of natural foods, with a wealth of quick and easy recipes clearly presented, with their ingredients described, and with reasons for their choice in preference to so-called 'convenience' processed foods. *This is the ideal book for all newcomers to natural foods.* Discover the FUN of healthy eating with EVELYN FINDLATER'S NATURAL FOODS PRIMER.

EVELYN FINDLATER'S
VEGETARIAN FOOD PROCESSOR

Quick and Easy Recipes to Make the Most of Your Machine

Vegetables need chopping. There is no getting away from this basic fact — yet vegetarianism does not HAVE to mean long hours tied to the kitchen sink, washing and preparing vegetables. **Evelyn Findlater** shows how to use a food processor to prepare delicious, healthy meals, quickly and simply. Sliced vegetables remain fresher and lose less vitamins when cut by the razor sharp blade of a processor; soups, purées and dips will be creamier without the addition of cream or butter; grains and nuts can be ground in record time, and batters, pastry and doughs become child's play — even baby foods can be made simply at home with the aid of a processor. Wholefoods and high technology thus form an unbeatable partnership in this excellent cookbook which explains, simply and clearly, everything you need to know about using a food processor.

THE VEGETARIAN COOKBOOK

Everything from Starters to Sweets

400 of the greatest variety of vegetarian meals you are ever likely to find anywhere.

Includes everything from Brazil Nut and Tomato Roast to Digestive Biscuits. **Doreen Keighley,** in conjunction with the Vegetarian Society of the United Kingdom, has here produced a superb collection of recipes tried and tested throughout many years of vegetarian cooking. She includes invaluable information on freezing the completed dishes and microwave defrosting as well as vital nutritional advice. Seasonal recipes such as Christmas Cake, Simnel Cake and Hot Cross Buns are treated to new invigorating recipes which are wholefood, vegetarian, high-fibre and low-fat and sugar and all are presented in a clear and easy-to-read style. *A great present — if you can bear to give it away!*

THE VEGETARIAN COOK BOOK 2

THE
VEGETARIAN COOK BOOK 2
More Delicious and Healthy Recipes for All Occasions
DAVID ENO

WITH BARBECUE RECIPES!

Co-published with the Vegetarian Society

More Delicious and Healthy Recipes for All Occasions

David Eno shows that the preparation of wholefoods is neither difficult nor time consuming — yet the results are delicious enough to tempt the appetite of even the most conservative eater! An essential guide to cooking and eating natural vegetarian foods, here is all the information you need about wholefood ingredients, their storage and preparation. Includes tempting recipes for all occasions, from breakfast through to tea-time and dinner, ***including barbecues.*** Produced in collaboration with the Vegetarian Society in the same highly successful format as The Vegetarian Cook Book.

NATURAL FOODS COOKBOOK

Marlis Weber. Everything you need to know about nourishing wholefoods including a 30 day menu plan. You will find a wealth of dishes for every meal and every occasion including energy-filled breakfasts, healthy office lunches and satisfying casseroles *plus* light and luscious desserts, breads, cakes and pastries made with wholegrains, nuts and dried fruits — and even ideas for delightful wholefood gifts! The recipes are all simple and straightforward, but flavour and nutrition are never sacrificed for simplicity and speed in this excellent wholefood cookbook.